THE TAIL
OF A
SALAMANDER

One Man's Journey To Save A Stream

Mark T. Wright, PhD, AIA, NCARB

where words connect

THE TAIL
OF A
SALAMANDER

One Man's Journey To Save A Stream

THE TAIL OF A SALAMANDER: *One Man's Journey To Save A Stream*

ISBN: 978-1-959811-34-3 (Paperback)
ISBN: 978-1-959811-35-0 (e-book)

Library of Congress Control Number: 2023924046

Cover Designer: Christina Panagiotis
Interior Design: Amit Dey
Illustrations and Photography: Mark T. Wright
Author and Cover Photo: Margaret Annie Wright

Published by Wordeee in the United States, Beacon, New York 2024

Website: www.wordeee.com
X Formerly Twitter: wordeeeupdates
Facebook: facebook.com/wordeee/
e-mail: contact@wordeee.com

Advance Praise

"A gorgeous book written by one of the most successful architects and planners in the United States. I love the book and clearly hear his voice. Powerful, enlightening, and out of the box. Mark T. Wright provides a new perspective that is desirable and smart."

—*Dr. John Hans Gilderbloom*
Multiple award-winning Environmental Rider
Professor, Department of Urban and Public Affairs
University of Louisville

"In *The Tail Of A Salamander* love is in the details and author Mark T. Wright gives them to us slowly, one wonder at a time. Fully embracing his conscious stewardship of the stream, we watch the blossoming of his children's self-awareness and reverence for all of life, human and non-human. Wright's writing style is as meandering and exploratory as the stream herself. We can hear, touch, and smell the North Carolina air. And with our entire being, we are heartened with a father's boundless, immeasurable love for his children."

—*Perri Neri*
Artist, Director of Living Room - NYC

"Each of us is on a journey of discovery. Dr. Wright brings us with him as he spends months bringing a stream, and himself, into balance. He finds that our lives, like his stream, are rarely straight lines; rather, they need meanders to find meaning, color, and hope. You won't regret taking this journey!"

—*R. L. Mullins Jr., PhD*
Author, Prairie Warbler
Co-author, Promise and Betrayal

"There is in a North Carolina mountain forest setting a work being done to restore 800 linear feet of a stream back to its eco-logical balance. Architect Mark Wright has documented this work in his wonderful new book, *The Tail Of A Salamander*. We read a day by day, sometimes hour by hour, documentation of his work over a several year span through poetic and historic narratives enlivened with humor and compelling anecdotes... all of which are charged with joy and meaning. Best of all, we find that he is joined in his pursuit by his two young children. The overall picture we get is of a true work of art which had been at the heart of Mark's initial intentions."

—*Tony Roccanova,*
Professor Emeritus
School of Architecture at the University of Kentucky

Dedication

For Margaret Annie and Harry

Prologue

The abbot retired from a Japanese monastery and decided to build a house in the mountains near a beautiful river where he could meditate and live out his days. The house built under extreme secrecy was rumored to be magnificent with splendid vistas of the river. Years later, on a day in spring when the river was beautiful from the spring rains, and with the work completed, the monks in the order received an invitation to visit the house and partake in a modest celebration. They started up the mountain and along a path lined with beautiful landscaping and elaborate stone. However, no one could see the water along the path or as they approached the front door. They were all welcomed and with great anticipation they thought the door would open, exposing a magnificent river view. As they entered the house, they were all perplexed, they still could not see the water. They began to mumble among themselves that the old monk had lost his mind to build a house in the mountains on the river but not to see it.

The celebration dinner was ready, and tradition was that all the guests would leave their shoes at the entry and wash their hands prior to eating. Each monk funneled through the foyer in single file and down a narrow dimly lighted hallway until they came to a fountain illuminated by a small low opening where they could wash their hands. They needed to bend down since the spicket was *low to the ground. As each one came to the fountain, they bent low, placed their hands under the spicket of lightly flowing water, and looked up. There, through a small window and between well-placed landscaping, they could see the river. As the water touched their hands, they saw the water of the river and realized the connection between the water on their hands and the water of the river and at the same time their grander connection and position in this universe.*

Old Chukka Boots
Pencil on Paper
Mark T. Wright

Mark T. Wright, age 3, 18th Street, Louisville, KY

Chapter I

7-1-21

As a young boy I lived in Louisville in the house built by my great great-grandfather, where the inner-city rear asphalt alley tributaries were my streams, and the streets were my rivers. I escaped the confines of that inner city environment, wonderful and full of adventure, but not the picturesque Louisville of Fitzgerald, commandeered the vehicle of education, and became an architect and later drove on to attain my PhD in planning. After I completed my first affordable housing project in the inner city of Louisville near the area where I grew up, my uncle said to me, "We are very proud of you, and it only took you thirty years to get ten blocks." That fondly ironic and humorous statement packed with unassuming wisdom, now resonates with me here in North Carolina where I live, and where it has only taken me an additional thirty-five years to get three hundred and fifty miles.

My journey began with a flyfishing trip to Montana near Glacier National Park and the Blackfoot river where I met a couple from Connecticut who had come out to Kalispel to float the river. Over breakfast, after exchanging pleasantries, they asked, "Why come all the way here? North Carolina is closer and the fishing is amazing. There's a guy there named Carl… with a guide service called Coast to…Something. Anyway, look it up, I think he's in Boone…we caught huge fish in a stream there." I had no answer except, "I didn't know."

Months later, I visited North Carolina to flyfish for trout with Carl Freeman, beginning my twelve-year quest for the mountain home. Since that first trip I had envisioned a place in the Carolina mountains where a stream runs through the property, where my children could experience the wonders in nature and where I could help in a small way to heal the planet and, little did I know at the time, heal myself. So, I bought a house in the mountains with a stream running through the southern eight-hundred-foot side of the nine-acre property. And like the inner-city alleys of my youth, the stream makes its way through the mountains and has been waiting to help guide me on my new and wondrous adventure.

The stream's journey begins, mountain spring fed, two miles west of the property at an elevation of three thousand feet above sea level. The stream flows west to east in an almost direct straight-line limping along through the property in an arduous effort to reach the nearest confluence of the main river. There is an elevation change of approximately ten feet across the property and a drop of one hundred feet further downstream at its termination. Before reaching the main river, the stream sports a sixty-foot-high waterfall two hundred yards from the confluence. The stream is a precious gift, alive and fickle, and after a gentle rain, it is impossible to over dream her soothing voice, as the stirring water sings a mystical timeless cascading lullaby perpetually echoing from mountain to mountain. Then the serenade quickly retreats, as it deflates and struggles with water flow, waiting for the next gentle rain shower to refresh and accelerate the current, amplifying the beautiful sound again. She is a perennial stream, but she struggles with balance.

Driving west to reach the property from the nearest city I pass the Cove Creek general store where I stop for eggs, the best chicken tenders on the planet, and local raw honey; the road leading to the old Cove Creek sawmill, twenty or so old tobacco barns, six horses, and six fields of cattle. After a short meandering scenic drive, I crossed the Watauga River. I leave the main highway turning onto a narrow gravel road that follows the contours of the stream, drive continuously up hill to reach the property, feeling the one-hundred-foot elevation change. In the dry summer months, the gravel road crunches beneath my wheels and seems to disappear mysteriously in my rear-view mirror in a surreal foggy cloud of fine limestone dust making me wonder if it will be there when I pass. This dust floats above the road drifting and swirling with the slight summer breeze, blanketing everything it touches with a grey limestone powder, but eventually sinks down dousing the lower area of the stream and landing on every exposed stone, tree and plant waiting to be washed away with the next rain. When walking in the stream, each step replicates this dust storm under water as a flash of silt stirs washing and dissipating downstream. A simple and real connection.

Bounded by mountains on one side and a sheer unguarded drop-off down to the stream on the other, there is no opportunity while driving the gravel road for relaxation, as close attention to the path at hand is paramount. The road begins exposed on the right side one hundred feet above the stream surface but reduces to ten feet when reaching the property. For anyone driving this road for the first time, the journey seems foreboding, and God forbid, the first experience navigating this gravel serpent is at nighttime when the normally peaceful climb becomes a victim of the mountain darkness; it is harrowing.

After this brief drive, passing one non-descript lonely and abandoned small white house and one ancient silent weathered grey tobacco barn, I crossed a short narrow bridge constructed of a steel superstructure and a wooden six by six planks surface. As I move slowly across, each board harmlessly tightening and adjusting to the weight of my vehicle then releasing as I pass, squeaks and moans like the ghost of an old man first waking in the morning with the aches of a lifetime. This is the artery and access, traversing the stream connecting the main gravel road to the lower section of the land and a driveway up to the house. The property, only thirty minutes from the nearest major city, still possesses a brilliant solitude and is majesty nestled in the bosom of the mountains.

During the day neighbors are within shouting range but seem to float quietly in the distance like smoke rings from a pipe behind dense mountain greenery. There are no fences between us; there is no need, and it feels as if there is an intuitive boundary of space we all respect. The trees, even when stripped naked by the fall winds, stand assembled across the mountain side shielding the house as enormous, staggered columns interrupting a precise view and become imposing but benevolent sentries guarding my privacy with a gauntlet of dark bark, wood, and root. At night, Taurus, Pisces, Sagittarius, and Aquarius, held with their kinfolk in a dense rich black sky free from light pollution, reveal deeper, more vivid patterns and layers I have never seen elsewhere. Even under this cloak of mountain darkness when seeing the water is difficult, the beautiful haunting sounds of the evening stream whisper to us through this temporary veil.

In 2004-2005 back-to-back hurricanes, Francis, then Katrina, saturated soils in the mountains to the brink. As a result, the stream flooded washing out the bridge, aided by timber from the Hansen's barn and a Volkswagen Beetle rushing downstream. The Hansen's contiguous property is upstream and directly west. Tom, a retired contractor and cabinet maker, and Liz a retired schoolteacher said, "it was a total mess, we've been here forty years and never saw anything like that, those back-to-back hurricanes in '05 and the road was completely under water. The bridge right out front, there at the road, gone too, maybe added to knocking yours out. The water came up to the front step, completely covered the pond out front, didn't it Tom." She pointed and Tom put his foot where the water stopped. "We were stuck here for a few days and had to go through Banner Elk to get anywhere until the state rebuilt the bridge."

"Really up that high?" I spoke.

It sure came close. Took the old barn but never made it into the house though. We were worried, then in the middle of the night we heard the crash and knew it was gone. That Volkswagen and probably the bridge out front, and God knows what else all took yours out?"

'Probably," I said.

"The state rebuilt the one out there and it's supposed to float up and take another flood, right Tom." Tom nodded his head in the affirmative. "At least that's what they said, but you

5

have a good one now. I remember when Wayne rebuilt your bridge. He graded the road up the hill there and we let him come through our property until they finished your bridge. That chain just unhooks."

"They could have built it just a wee bit wider," I said.

They are good people, who know these mountains, who raised two girls here, who are educated and peaceful, and who were kind enough to allow the previous owner to excavate an access road through to their property while the bridge across the stream to this property was being reconstructed. They have been kind to me.

Laurel Creek and The Cottage at Laurel Creek

The current bridge rebuilt that same year with its steel superstructure six feet higher than the original, about eight feet off the water, seems to challenge and taunt and tempt the stream with tenuous defiance to rise and take it again during every heavy rain and stream swell. Concrete remnants of the previous bridge litter the water lodged in the bowels of the stream as large rectangular slabs protruding like massive dorsal fins above the surface. Other concrete islands litter and mingle with the stones along the stream edges. They have become permanent fixtures altering the course of the water the same as their distant cousins, the rocks, and the boulders. At only eighteen years old these slabs of concrete, infants compared to the timeless age of the boulders, welcomed by the other stones, integrate into the internal intricate workings of the stream. They are integral in shaping the form of the stream while at the same time yielding to the eroding wetness of the stream family, and as the rocks and boulders sometimes are, victims of the water's wrath. Just as the stream water smooths the rocks and boulders, it wears on these giant slabs attempting to free and expose the small stones from their Portland cement captor, much like the water exposing the stones on the stream bottom. These slabs, manmade, now absorb the energy of the water.

The house is forty years old, built from lumber harvested on the property and milled just two miles up the road at the old, abandoned Cove Creek mill. The timber structure is also alive and creaks and pops ,and moves and shifts, and contracts and expands, breathing as the stream does with the weather changes. This is the architectural language I speak fluently and have been translating to anyone who will listen for forty years. The house needs considerable work but is livable and sets midway up the mountain about one hundred feet above the stream. During the day and on clear evenings lit by a full moon, from the south porch and from the kitchen window, as I stand in front of the sink facing south, washing dishes, washing hands, and making tea, I can see parts of the stream regardless of the season.

Most dawns, if the fog has not saturated the landscape fully, in a syncopated cyclic dance, the sun struggles to slowly escape the imposing pine tree capped mountain top an hour or so after it has risen above the eastern lower planes, but still manages to lightly illuminate the enthralling scene below while the mountain life begins to stir. This is the beauty of the mountain sunrise. There is no abrupt intrusion from a fiery star. Instead, there is a restrained transition and gentle tease into the light of day. As I witness this phenomenon, I sip my cup of tea each morning, made from well water and brewed from loose leaf tea, I turn my head and bend my ear toward the open kitchen door, slow my breathing and beg to listen to the distant continuous soothing sound of the stream penetrating every cell of the house.

I am bombarded by magnificent distractions of nature rousing to meet each new morning. The random rustling and graceful flicker of the leaves on loan to the birches until fall; the rapid tap, tap, tap of the downy woodpecker; the Morse-code-like like...caw, caw...caw, caw of black as tar crows, lock stepping across a small green clearing searching for breakfast; the does and brown speckled fawns cautiously foraging heads down for clover, then heads up and ears perked, then down again; the stream's apex predator in its disguise as a small black mink, cute and curious playfully skimming the stream sides for prey; a blue heron with its head snake-like cocked motionlessly stalking and waiting to strike chubs from a boulder perch in the center of the stream; the herd of ladybugs lounging in the upper left corner of the east facing window; and a grey ground squirrel frantically licking the red nectar splashed on the top of the porch rail from the sloppiness of two hummingbirds sampling the hung feeder.

With pleasant inexplicable deliberateness, I avoid indulging these wonders and gaze slowly down the mountain side across the small grassy clearing bordering the stream and onto the bank touching the water. There, inside the remaining mist magically hovering above the water, the Naiads of the enchanted stream call to me with a sumptuous invitation from these dancing nymphs to join them in a celebration. The stream draws me to her with a magnetic, hypnotic sense of wonder, and like the visceral irresistibility to cut and taste warm freshly baked bread the minute it comes from the oven. And with every tick of the hallway clock and every delightful sip of tea, I connect with the stream, the land and the house, and somehow know she has been waiting for me so we may help each other to heal and fully live again.

What began as a concern about losing three birch trees to heavy flooding and erosion along the stream bank, and concerns about stagnant water holding gnats and mosquitos, evolved into a mission and an adventure to restore the stream. So, along with renovating the house and the cottage, I decided to restore and revive the stream, helping her to become more in balance. I see the stream, the bridge, the house, the cottage, and the land as overlapping elements of a symbiotic ecosystem drawing life from each other and not thriving unless they all thrive. But the stream passing through the land as veins returning blood through the body, is the life force among us all. As I feel the water flowing through the stream, it is like a transfusion detoxifying the harmful energy in my soul.

After researching technical data, case studies, and academic articles from a multitude of entities outlining stream restoration, fluvial geomorphology, trout behavior, entomology, and native riparian plant life, I planned. But therein lies two grand illusions. Research and defining something do not allow for a fuller deeper understanding. There is no substitute for "doing." And if you are not completely flexible and bend like a willow, the journey will become frustrating and clouded. As that great sage, Mike Tyson said about boxing, "Everybody has a plan until they get punched in the face." The victor thinks on his feet. The stream is alive and fluid and as the Taoist does, the practice and the doing will reveal the soul of the plan. But make no mistake, nature can be an unpredictable pugilist and will not hesitate to punch you in the face.

I practice in the water with this amazing object of nature, face-to-face, innocent and sincere, sculpting the stream as a vessel for the water, using only hand tools and trying to use only the materials already deposited there and limiting the work within the confines of the existing stream bed and banks. In the end this may be a fool's errand, but I must try. There is an intimacy missed, and a sacred trust violated if large machinery intruded in the process, or of others involved who cannot hear her voice or feel her "pilgrim soul." True, the work is arduous and sometimes overwhelming, but it is my own, fulfilling even in my failures. Being in the water, I become part of the stream, approachable and indivisible from the life surrounding me. It is as if the wildlife sees me as non-human or they recognize my intrusion poses no danger to them. The mink, which is mostly nocturnal, has seen me so often he comes to me closer each time curious and friendly. The hummingbirds come to me hovering at eye level so close I can hear their wings beat. The deer cross the stream near me unperturbed as if I am another boulder. The water snakes hover on the surface at my heels, head up, waiting for me to disturb the rocks shaking lose their next meal.

I do not expect others to take on a mantle of this magnitude or join my quest in total and mobilize with shovels in hand to move boulders, clean and help revive a stream. And others, who have never stood transparent in any waters, see this as an indulgence when there is according to them, "a priority to get other things done to generate income." Still others look upon moving rocks around with your bare hands as an exercise in futility washed away during the next flood. I offer them no explanation or excuse for the timing and schedule of all the work, and only hope clarity reaches them when they experience the sound of flowing water, because it is impossible to stand in the middle of a stream and not feel the consciousness of imagination rising in your soul. I offer no new knowledge or attempt to discuss the science of fluvial geomorphology or stream hydrodynamics. If the reader learns something, then it is because they have looked inward. And if anything can make one a poet; it is the stream. But others might live vicariously through me here, taking whatever sip they choose, or sample they might need, to glean from the cool healing water I present. This is a narrow and personal journey as I attempt to learn everything about the stream and in so doing, learn more about myself. There is a short story about two young monks, Yoshi, and Ki, who were walking along a stream.

> *"Look at the fish playing in the stream so happily," said Yoshi. "How do you know what the fish are feeling you are not a fish," said Ki. "How do you know I do not know," said Yoshi.*

Fish and Salamanders Playing
Pencil, pen and ink on paper
Mark T. Wright

As Gaston Bachelard explained, "We believe naively that we need only to speak of an object to think that we are being objective. However, as the story above illustrates the two realities, choosing to experience the object reveals more about us than we do about it." The surrealist poet Paul

Eluard pleaded, "We must not look on reality as being like ourselves." Einstein called it an "optical delusion," separating ourselves and our reality from the rest of the universe and a prison where we must escape. Chuang-Tse explained, "A well frog cannot imagine the ocean, nor a summer insect the winter." So we cannot understand the stream if we restrict ourselves by narrowing our perspective. And as Mark Twain puts it, "I have no problem with education unless it gets in the way of learning." Then the brilliant educator, Joseph Campbell raved from his mythical magical pulpit, "There is only one unpardonable sin...the one of not being alert, not quite awake."

If we do not escape our own prejudicial prison of perception, our perspective becomes closed, arrogant, deaf, dangerous, and quite frankly, boring. The experience of doing, of being in and around the water, is severely personal and mystical, intensely symbolic, limited by my own experience as a neophyte, and becomes Proustian and Taoist, often charging memories and thoughts that seem vastly unconnected, but in fact are the purest example of connectivity. If we are locked into certain realities, such as the scientist, the ecologist, the architect, the biologist, the adult, the hydrologist, the engineer, the angler, the social scientist, the romantic, the poet, the academic, the artist, the entomologist, the builder; we fail to realize the similarities and intimate common connections among us and fail to understand that the language of the stream and the water as multilingual and universal. I offer the following extrapolation on a traditional Zen koan:

A Zen master stood by a stream in front of his students. "If you call this a stream, you are denying its reality. If you do not call it a stream, you deny the fact. Now, tell me, what do you call this?"

This amazing phenomenon of nature is determined to survive without my ragged and well-intentioned intervention in an unpredictable unbalanced form. But, if we become aware, and bend our soul's ear toward the water, we hear her speak to us, in a language we initially do not understand, that sounds hauntingly familiar, and that we need to learn. She can instruct us gracefully, laughs at us often, consoles us sometimes and suggests recompense for our transgression against her. By attempting to learn her language and reflecting on ours, and accepting our responsibility as stewards of her well-being, we begin to understand what we need to do. It is this continuous conversation with the stream that draws me and drives me to devote the effort to the work of restoring this beautiful broken and fragile creature to balance. It is the doing that allows us both to grow and connects me to the stream. There's a Chinese proverb, "Learn to do one thing well and you will know how to do all things."

I have searched for enlightenment as a practicing architect for over forty years and with each project have escaped my own prejudicial prison of perception by practice. In the case of resurrecting and restoring this stream I must first learn a new language as an infant learns and takes on the language of their parents before having their own voice. Then I will be able to have an initial and continuous conversation with the water, the negative space that we call the stream which confines the water and is its inseparable partner, the boulders, the rocks, the pebbles the gravel, the sand, and the silt, the flora, the air, but also attempt to think as a brook trout, a crayfish, a salamander, and the insects that I hope will thrive here. This is my reality and my privileged conversations with the stream to find a new architecture for the present. "How do you know I don't know?"

Rerouted water flow, upstream view.

Chapter II

7-19-21

The rain fell slowly at the beginning carried on the backs of unassuming clouds sneaking over the dark green pine and fir trees atop the western Carolina Mountain range. It marched down and across the lower mountain area on a gentle unassuming zephyr suppressing the sun as it moved east first wetting the darker evergreens at the upper elevations, then the light green deciduous trees midway up the mountains and finally began to tickle the olive-colored leaves of the birch trees at the lower level lining the stream edge. It was midday but felt as if the lightest of breezes blew behind it over the lower elevations an enormous sailboat casting its imposing shadow on a small mountain dinghy, bringing an early faux darkness. Nannie would have said, "The devil is beatin' his wife," since there was still stubborn sunshine in front of the moving grey shadows while it was raining.

The stream has not yet felt the needed rebaptism and is sadly suffering from a sickeningly slow current and straight eroded widened edges encouraging the water temperature to rise during the summer dry season, suppressing its life energy. There is an innate struggle between sun and stream when the sun stimulates this shallow slow-moving water heating the surface, to the delight of the insects, but accelerating its evaporation. The stream, aided by shade from the bank plants and trees, desperately resists the rising surface temperature but finally succumbs and reluctantly begins to give up the liquid water to vapor. There is an absence of deep holes and deeper runs, of riffles that oxygenate and cool the water, and areas where every sentient entity such as, fish, small minnows, salamanders, crayfish, and water snakes could hold, as the result of the widened straight stream pattern and a risen stream bottom center. Unhealthy debris spotted along the edges, stuck in time and boulders, such as old mattress pieces, refrigerator parts, discolored dirty plastic bottles and shoes, pieces from junked cars right down to the seat foam cushions and rusted leaf springs, litter the banks. The stream has become old and frail, stiff and inflexible, barely breathing, barely moving, aching and less elastic. She has become more easily bruised, recovering from trauma more slowly and is at the mercy of the water occurring in extremes.

The air is heavy with gnats hovering above the small shallow stagnant pools swarming to my every exhale, every eyelid blink and still head. I make sure my yellow bandanna is tucked inside the back of my hat and placed over ears, mouth, and nose under my glasses to avoid invasion from these tiny creatures. They still move and land under my glasses as if they need a better enlarged view through my spectacles. A quick upward exhale puff blows them away temporarily. Water striders gathered below each swarm facing upstream breast stroking with their middle legs, effortlessly scooting in quick short sprints strategically repositioning continuously.

They are hoping for a mistake from the flying insects that may inadvertently kiss the water becoming easy pickens' for this agile and entertaining predator that does not break the water surface tension. Small biting flies and mosquitos that have made it past the striders as larvae now hover over still water and become joyous in their holding spots along the bank ready to pounce on any bare skin.

The tree canopy shields the initial raindrops from reaching the stream as they begin lightly tapping the birch, walnut, tulip poplar and oak leaves. I can still sit on a huge dry boulder under the canopy adjacent to the stream and hear the droplets hitting the trees but notice nothing is striking me. I feel the same innocent anticipation as I did as a child sitting on Nannie's front porch watching a storm approaching over the city houses and buildings. The rain evokes an indelible memory of the smell of wet rooftops and asphalt streets, the sounds of automobile tires rolling wet in the street, the color deepening on concrete walks and small patches of greenspaces, washed by the rain as I sat dry on the loggia.

Birds have become hidden and still. The pair of eastern phoebes, nesting under the house overhang, earlier were excitedly active, scurrying in a relay of flight with food for their three hatchlings, knowing they are down from rain soon. The flying insects are thinning out replaced by the thickened humid air and darkening sky acting as a harbinger that the coming storm is not simply a benign passing mountain shower. The remaining flies and mosquitos have migrated to my shielded location for the last dry shelter and a hopeful meal. The clouds push quickly east, now stealing the sun more rapidly, keeping the devil's wife safe.

Unseen upstream, western portions of the mountain feel the rain first occurring minutes earlier. This lower section of the stream suffers the accumulation of the rain as it moves downstream to my location, as well as the effects of runoff from my land, house, and drive in real time. Additional runoff upstream not absorbed by the land from driveways, and roofs on houses, barns and sheds owned by the Averys, the Gunners, the Howells, the Hansens, the Stablers, the Moores, the Kennedys, the Roberts, the Funderburkes, the Apostolic Missionary Baptist church, snowball and add to the volume of water. As the upstream water moves to me with a snowballing effect, it is as if I am witnessing the weight of light from a star reaching me that burned eons ago translated into the language of the stream. The rain is increasing, and I begin to see droplets banking off the birch limbs, skirting through open spaces in the canopy, spotting my green shirt, tapping the brim of my hat, washing the grey limestone road dust off the lower plants allowing them to shine with reflecting wetness and reaching the stream surface. My front porch boulder shelter begins to degrade and leak. The surrounding land shows a glistening of moisture, only touching the tops of the grasses and not yet saturating the soil below.

The rain drops hit the stream surface creating countless shallow interlocking dimples in a desperate attempt to revive her. The view of the stream bottom below the shallow and clear water slowly becomes distorted, made blurry by the rain hitting the surface. The initial light rain helps increase the current slightly washing across the stream bottom and there is hope of resurrection from a gentle shower blessing the stream bed. Her corridor is wide, increasing her capacity for water but she has lost the ability to transport sediment away and is now straight, showing continuous scars caused by extreme flooding as nothing impedes the water's erosive destructive energy. Her center belly has risen from years of accumulated gravel, debris, sand and silt and the stream edges have deepened resembling the edge gutters of the old gravel road above. There is no center channel and there is more sediment deposited in the stream than it can transport downstream. Her surface area has reluctantly increased while her depth has decreased encouraging more rapid evaporation while her diversity dwindles and normal water flow is nonexistent in spots, excruciatingly slow, shallow, and barely reaching depths of one inch and less except for a deep spot under the bridge. A trickle of current randomly crosses the scattered pebbled bottom in braided patterns creating an uneven San Marco like floor, appearing as millions of wavey multicolored earth tone smooth mosaic tiles refracting the light by the passing water interrupted only by the dots of randomly dispersed rocks and boulders. I say there is an inch of water, but the pebbles are between an inch and an inch and a half in diameter and the water flows mostly between them barely piercing the top levels of the stones.

Ceramic Mosaic by Nancy LaChapelle

We appear to mimic Jesus' walking on the water at the Sea of Galilee when we walk atop these gems as the stream passes between them and under our feet at a slow tattered laborious pace only disturbed by our footprints leaving temporary testament with depressions and eerily dispersed silt moving away downstream with the struggling shallow current. This peaceful shallowness permeates the stream route as an inconspicuous condition and on its own is another constant reminder of a stream out of balance. The rain is picking up.

Birch tree leaves begin to flex down, down, down from the weight of accumulated raindrops, then after spilling their gathered water, flex up quickly to repeat looking like an elegant bamboo Japanese garden water feature; others move with random flutter twisting side to side as the rain drops begin to hit the leaves with intensity. Droplets are sneaking through the canopy more frequently and hitting the stream surface. The ground is beginning to saturate and soon contributes water to the stream volume as run off. The air begins to cool smelling like dirt and nightcrawlers invited from their underground lairs by the moist surface, later becoming involuntary smorgasbord for the attentive crows. The rain lays down the dust from the adjacent limestone gravel road ten feet above the stream on the south side, and the road absorbs the water slowly as it also saturates before it sheds to the stream.

The Gunners have driven down the mountain to the bank of six standard galvanized steel mailboxes mounted on wooden posts near the bridge, consolidating mail for several homes in the immediate area up the mountain, with daily clockwork to retrieve the day's delivery then vanish up the mountain minutes before the next vehicle arrives. The 3:15 p.m. yellow school bus tattooed with the Watauga County logo along its side, making its last stops, squeals its brakes, guns its engine, rotates out the 'stop' sign on its hinges on the driver's side like a red flashing door perpendicular to the side of the bus, cranks open its front bifold passenger side doors with a hydraulic hiss, drops off a few neighborhood children quickly. It is my benchmark of time for the day, and other than the position of the sun, is my only clock when I am in the stream. The Stabler children met by their waiting grandmother run to the small white one-story modest house to avoid a soaking. The bus speeds off past me banging, bumping, rattling, jostling every front wheel ball joint unable to avoid the minefield of scattered and continuous potholes confined by the gravel road, and stirring the last weak bit of wetted dust behind it mixing with the thick smell of diesel exhaust; the last bit of dust before the rain tamps it fully down. The rain has picked up.

The tree canopy no longer shields the stream. My shirt has been transformed from light olive to a darker wet green and the rain is slowly rolling off my hat brim after tapping it in unsynchronized rhythm amplifying the sound of each wet strike as if my head were covered by a hollow drum. I am hoping the rain provides only a slight soaking of these mountains that gently and graciously breathes renewed life into the struggling stream. The clouds have completely engulfed the sun, and the upper dark green trees in the distance, seen through imposing raindrops and drifting mist appear muted and hazy. Animals and insects have universally retreated to safer dry positions anticipating heavier rain. The gravel road, resembling the profile of the unhealthy stream below, crested in its middle, now saturated, and has begun shedding water to its lower side edges and into main galvanized corrugated steel pipe collectors before depositing the water into the stream. The water mixed with the loose suspended limestone fines of the road fill the edge gravel gutters, creating a milky grey liquid moving downhill, migrating into the stream. It then drifts downstream and across the mosaic stream bed like a desert sandstorm transforming the clear water into a stone-colored flowing mass moving more rapidly with the increased current. The color is slightly grey as the runoff only raises the water an inch or so at this point while the rocks and boulders are still sticking their heads above the surface as black random dots scattered against the solid-colored greyish fluid canvas background. The rain has picked up.

As the volume of water increases exponentially, fed from rain upstream compounding the rain received in this stretch of stream, the water level begins to rise rapidly and unabated. I cannot help but think the clouds would stop their tears much earlier if they knew that they cannot save the stream alone and that they may unintentionally contribute to her continued demise. But as it stands, they feel no obligation to temper their rush of water as the heavy shower assault continues. We are witnessing the most simple, real, and direct example of the butterfly effect. The rain picks up yet again as the sky darkens and the now ominous charcoal clouds remain stubborn, seeming to stall directly over the stream determined to stay put. I am astonished how the speed of the current has increased in the last few minutes, resembling an expressway of fast-moving water instead of a quiet alley, and how quickly the water level is rising. I put on my rain jacket, left my boulder, traversed the still relatively shallow stream bed, and made my way up the northern bank to a higher safer stream edge. The rain picks up.

The deluge begins miles upstream, a swelling dynamo, fueled by every rain droplet shedding off every impervious surface built over the last one hundred years, increasing exponentially as it moves downstream allowing nothing to impede or escape its punishment and the stalwart energy and acceleration. The straightened stream shape, degraded edges, and shallow depth with no center channel offer no relief and cannot absorb the rampage of the explosive gurgling energy as the water spreads out immediately wide from edge to edge. After years of valiant effort, the edges cannot resist the water's pounding discharge and has relinquished and succumbed to sheared and undercut banks. The torrent moves downstream tumbling boulders and covering every tree and bush with now brownish grey-green violent water. I cannot recognize the original stream banks somewhere submerged, usurped by the swirling foaming water that has risen two feet in a matter of hours, and now rushing uncontrollably in a perfectly straight line.

The stream bottom is no longer discernable, and the power of the water is terrifyingly hypnotic. The soothing sound of cascading water has escalated to a brilliant frightening pervasive roar devouring, engulfing, and overpowering any other sounds. I feel an uneasy rumbling from the heart of the rushing water sending vibrations striking my body as a floating shock wave. The same wave travels along the banks migrating through the conduit of the earth rattling the soles of my feet. I am careful not to approach the stream edges, although drawn to the destructive force and the horrible new form that the stream takes. The rain continues overnight and into the next late morning pounding the metal roof of the house like a timpani drum adding to the unyielding roar of the flooded stream. The stream has risen three feet engulfing the corrugated road drainage pipes, backwashing water up the pipes onto and over the road. The bottom flange of the 'I' beam bridge structure is only five feet above the water surface and is a highway used by the squirrels as they scurry across to escape any danger.

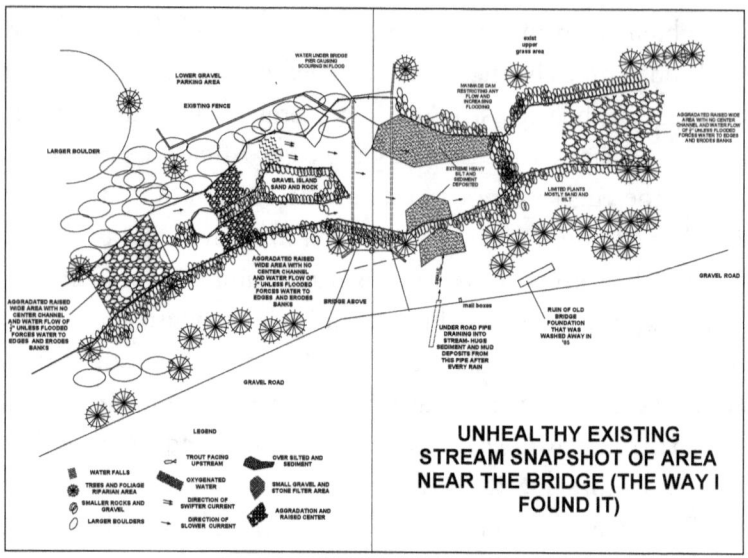

UNHEALTHY EXISTING STREAM SNAPSHOT OF AREA NEAR THE BRIDGE (THE WAY I FOUND IT)

The small bridge shows cautious contempt for the rising flood waters remembering the fate in 2005 of its predecessor when the water did not discriminate with its destruction. The deluge stops short of quarreling with the bridge and the roaring dragon will not devour the structure this time, but the piers supporting the structure, engulfed by the inflated stream, are tested. I think of the stories my grandmother told me of the 1937 flood when the Ohio River rose and overwhelmed the city of Louisville. Then, she was pregnant with my mother, and as the water rose engulfing the first floor of the house on 18th Street she was rescued from the roof of the front porch in a small boat. The main street was a literal river. Nothing is absolute.

Flora that has grown above the stream limits, where the flood has not reached yet, obscures the view of the stream from the road. It has crept down the banks sparsely near the stream boundary; softening the edges, adding shade, and cooling the water surface in summer while struggling to protect the stream edges from the timeless tumultuous deterioration. However, the lower green seasonal plant blanket of the riparian area, now submerged holding its breath, is not an adequate cover anchor or protector, and erosion continually widens the stream sides harshly and with purpose. The rain had finally stopped by midmorning, but the results of the water's rampage continued to deliver the destruction from upstream for twelve more hours.

The stream quickly returns to its tortured lower water level in a few days. The unbridled ferocity of the flooding reveals the ravaged, flattened, feathered, ragweed, oatgrass and chain ferns lying pummeled and forced in the direction of the flood waters along the limited riparian area. This area of vegetation, when healthy, between the aquatic and terrestrial worlds, provides cover for wildlife; helps reduce erosion and helps filter the ground water entering the stream. Debris deposited violently from miles upstream, has landed stuck behind boulders, pinched between groups of rocks, and is scattered along the stream edges marking the upper elevation and line of the event. Three feet above the normal stream bottom carved straight and wide, the turbulent action of the water undercuts and exposes the roots of the magnificent birch trees, lining the eroded bank edges as defenseless soldiers in formation, desperately clinging with skeleton like fingers of determination to the remaining eroded soil. Three birches have fallen. The heavy rain is no friend to the straight earth edges, using the widened flat stream to funnel and concentrate rushing water stealing any wealth of soil from the banks. The stream exists in extremes as nature holds a sword of Damocles above her head.

Refuse clean up by Harry and Margaret Annie.
Oh, the rubbish they found!

Chapter III

The long days of summer had been compressing the night, but beginning a month ago they have loosened their grip on the daylight and the days are shortening. Daybreak brought thick low clouds sandwiching the sunrise between the heavens and the mountains, restricting morning light reflecting off the underbelly ceiling of the sky. I completed my early morning ritual practicing Qigong, took a sip of tea before I began work on the stream, and reflected on the peaceful movement outside my southeast window dotted with spider webs, a small brownish tulip moth, and a delicate skinny green grasshopper lounging on the screen waiting for the sun to warm them. I drifted to moments wading and fly-fishing another small stream nearby named Helton Creek. On occasion, there in the stream, as it does here, the work and the casts would cease, and the surrounding mountains would consume me. For priceless moments I dream, induced by nature and all evidence of time vanishes as I witness events that have repeated over countless lifetimes. I believe it was Thoreau who said that man invented fishing as an excuse to be in and on the water.

The breeze, funneling, tumbling down the angled banks, unfurling at the water's edge, then following the stream channel and vibrated the rhododendron leaves along the banks to a spectacular frenzied flutter like thousands of green butterflies perched on overhanging limbs. I watched the wind travel the stream corridor toward me as far as the next bend allowed and witnessed the graceful movement of the leaves occurring in waves as if they were scudding along the banks toward me. The vague scent of earth and water rides on the wake of the warm zephyr overwhelmingly saturated with the pungent thick musty fragrance of honeysuckle.

A lake or pond exhibits rhythmic movement in the presence of a breeze, resulting in waves and ripples upon its previously sedentary surface. We wonder if the wind is enticing and tickling the energy inherent in the water, waking, and encouraging it to rise and dance, or if the still water has yielded and succumbed to the induced energy of the breeze allowing it to drive the action. Undeniably, on a previously sedentary body of water this partnership creates a pleasant rhythmic motion on the surface. But picture the gracefully flowing water formed by the confines of the stream banks moving in the opposite direction as the breeze in magnificent dissonance, unencumbered and oblivious to the air movement, refracting images pierced with dappled sunlight dancing at its own pace, and we witness a frantic complicated complex chaotic and glorious composition affecting and inundating our senses. Stravinsky in nature. I reflected on that transcendent moment as the water reflected and mirrored the movements of the leaves, adding the rippling effect of the water fluid and unyielding, doubling the number of joyful flutters.

I embraced the image of my children's first excursion to experience the beauty of the artful practice of fly fishing.

Donned in their tiny waders, ball caps and rain jackets, they walked with me into the stream while clutching my hand. We walked carefully into the stream center, rod in my left hand while they vise-gripped my right hand as we moved together with simple, slow deliberate steps on the slippery rocks below our boots. We do not realize the unyielding and extraordinary strength and vigilance that a child has while holding your hand when they are unsure of the surroundings. I normally cast with my right hand, but the small fingers refused to loosen their hold since the water level moved around my knees but flowed to their crotch. So, I gladly taught myself to cast left-handed and proceeded. Grateful anglers caught rainbow, brown and brook trout, which were touched by tiny hands, admired with wonder, thanked for their time, then released. We built riverbed dams of pebbles around elaborate sandcastles for armies of superheroes with found sticks for shovels, knowing these were beautiful sand paintings absorbed by the next rains. Small hands heaved rocks into the water for the simple joy of the splash, and turned over larger rocks gently finding snails, nymphs, and crawdads. We laughed at our clumsiness on slippery rocks, as I told them stories of my many stumbles and falls, and I listened to glorious stories of pirates, transformers, and Star Wars.

One more sip and now to work with all.

There is an old Irish saying, "No field ever got ploughed by talking about it." Thus, "the doing" becomes a necessary condition, as much as the planning, in order to speak and understand the stream language. I have been working on the stream now for four months and have established a new reinforced and simple bank structure outlined and developed for three hundred feet of the approximately eight hundred feet of stream. The work in general, takes on three lives after the meditative observing and initial planning:

1. The chaotic major clearing and cleaning of unhealthy debris.
2. The general sculpting, and the refining with input from the stream and water.
3. Fine tuning with minor ongoing maintenance.

These do not exist independently and occur continuously sometimes in random order as nature helps mold the stream. The hope is the clearing, cleaning, refining, and tuning occurs occasionally, and the meditative observing is continuous for a lifetime.

Two days ago, the area received four inches of rain in twenty-four hours; a gully washer that flooded the stream making it rise about three feet above normal. When the deluge subsided there appeared a deliberate scarification of taller grass mowed down and brushed in the downstream direction; a rat's nest of newly toppled trees dangling in the current; piles of debris lodged behind now exposed boulders stacked in random order on top of each other, and a bold message for me with a clear map to reframe the bank.

While the water level approached its crest, the stream revealed her resolve to resist the force of the deluge. But she eventually and reluctantly became resigned to the roaring destructive pervasive power of the water as the fluid volume became insufferable for the normal faux stream banks to contain, resulting in the flood waters overwhelming her and cutting new even wider edges. The violent action of the rushing unimpeded water inside the temporarily swelled stream borders etched more extreme scars into the stream side earthen skin. Quietly observing and solemnly studying this extreme event, even in its apparent negativity, revealed clues that may assist her in embracing and absorbing this violent energetic indiscretion from nature when she can no longer accommodate and confine the deluge. Witnessing this period and the comparatively deafeningly silent aftermath, it is frighteningly obvious the stream and its immediate surroundings are an integral and indispensable part of nature, and at the same time a vulnerable and independent victim.

Stream
Mixed Media
Mark T. Wright and Perri Neri

After the deluge, areas of the new work were rendered irrelevant when the flooding waters pummeled the rocks and overflowed the banks, and the myth of Sisyphus seemed a reality. The less affected areas were those with a lower degree of bank slope which allowed the stream to gently widen and overflow absorbing the violent energy of the flood waters. But this was a lesson. This was a clear and violent parameter spoken in nature's language to contend with: not to fight, not to try to predict the total effect, but to plan for its occurrence. I thought about a story.

One day, while walking along a path above the local river, a group of people and their guide were observing the wonderful power of the rapids and churning water below. Suddenly, they saw an old frail looking man jump into the water just above the roaring rapids. The group panicked and hurried down the to the water in hopes to save the old man. They reached a spot well below the rapids where the water was calmer and to their surprise saw the old man emerge from the water and slowly walk to shore toward them unharmed. The group was astonished that the old man survived the rapids. The guide approached him, "How did you survive those rapids? We came down to help you and were terrified that you drowned."

The old man replied, "I have been swimming in these waters since I was a boy almost fifty years now. Over that time, I have learned the temper of the river. The water level changes often from rain and drought, but the principal temper of the river stays the same. I have learned not to fight the river. I jump in and when the river goes up, I let it take me up and when the water goes down, I go with it, but I never struggle against the current. You will not win. Only by embracing the temper of the river's action and giving into its force will you survive the swim."

The rain stopped and the next day the water began to recede. The stream spoke to me of her wish and method for recovery and healing. The flow became strong but still harsh, but a movement of brilliance and a language began to show. The second day with no rain, the current slowed again, to where I could begin to read the flooded high-water level and the way the stream tried to recover. We began a conversation of creativity and a plan. The third day after the rain stopped, the best day, the flowing water became consistent, where the stream began to recover and show its independence from the water teasing it in the directions she desired and hinting at its preferred path. The fourth day with no rain, and no extreme intrusions, the water flow decreased again, and the stream began to show undefined boundaries and confusing conflicting paths. The fifth day with no rain the water flow decreased yet again the stream reverted to its struggling shallow low widened scarred and painfully slow water level.

Every damn dam I dismantle, every rock and boulder I move and place by hand, resulted in me hardly able to move my arms without pain. I fear I have damaged a tendon in my right-hand middle finger from the shovel pounding it continuously. It now locks up when I bend my finger. I have destroyed three pairs of heavy leather gloves and have ordered a different type of rubberized glove designed for masonry work to test its durability. I feel like I have rubbed the fingerprints from my fingers managing the stones. Discretion is not my forte when I am embraced by the water, and I am taken beyond what I thought I was physically able to accomplish.

There is calmness in the stream that dissolves frantic illusions such as doubt, hatred, and negativity by the simple actions of cascading water and gravity. There are no feelings of loneliness in the stream. Thoughts and dreams become reassuring partners. The work warms me. Failures and successes fade and washed in holy water, disappear downstream as insignificant particles of silt. The past and future dissolve and only the present exists, and I realize the efforts here are sand paintings in the relative pocket of time. Hurtful memories of musty hotel rooms with bookless shelves; misguided loyalty and conviction; betrayals and over held morality, pointless conversations of anger; loss and grief creep in slithering over and between the rocks and boulders like slick algae drifting painlessly downstream with the ruffled sediment. Old friends, old lovers, first breaths and small first faces, and the joy of small visits, small shoes, about 1,440 sunsets and leaf boats carrying away all regrets; my dear old friend JD, and the music of James Brown and dancing when no one else would, are images that float to me continuously, repeating like the magical cycle of the water.

The history of the stream asks me questions I cannot answer. I can only respond in reference to the history that I have made. In the stream I become a conduit connecting earth, atmosphere, and water, grounded to the bedrock, and like the chimney in the Robbie house, driven as a stake from the hand of God down through the heart of the house holding it from floating and shifting apart. The sky sits atop the water, which moves atop the earth channel, and I feel like one of the protruding boulders in the stream redirecting current while connecting elements. The sins of my fabricated world wash away downstream with judgement reserved for stupidity, not sincere failed attempts. Enemies real and dreamed drift away with ego and self-contempt as the lightest silt.

The stream feels like an old friend and our many lives have intermingled since time. There are no worrisome clock faces staring at me, only moments too real to explain and too mystical to believe. Every instance in the water contributes to a renewed life flourishing pure and cleansed from the soiled preface of my flawed humanity. The stream is quenching the red-hot beaten metal of the last twenty years, reconfiguring the molecules of my soul, allowing those imposters of ego, forgiveness, and fear, to skirt as easily with a *zing* across the steel surface as a file across a hardened blade. The rebaptism of the spirit in holy water becomes a reality, not simply a metaphor, but at the same time metaphor. Physical work helps me absolve worthless decisions and creates a world of healing through burning muscles extinguished with water.

I often sit quietly in the middle of the stream on a huge, exposed boulder watching every delightful dance of current and animal unfold before me, every line of heavenly poetry performed by the water, and listen to every note sung by the stream waiting to be composed into music. In my solitude there, the voice of the stream sometimes screams with such force the boulders bow down before her, Cleopatra of the mountains, and animals stagger in a drunken stupor. Such is the power of the water.

I have found ways to move boulders I thought I could not by using the assistance of the current, by lever, by DaVinci, by Archimedes, by Newton, by pivoting them on other stones, and by spit and a prayer. The stream is very shallow, yet somehow my boots fill with water, my trousers become soaked and sagging. I forget to eat and drink, to stop except to study the next move which is dependent on the previous which changes the last. The study is critical. Listening is paramount. The intimate observation is joyful. The execution is arduous. The practice is.

7-30-21

About two miles west, just up from the Cove Creek store, I found heavy machinery parked in the middle of Cove Creek. The Resource Institute is undertaking the complete revival and efficient working of a 2,000 feet section of Cove stream to reduce erosion and stabilize stream boundaries. Massive boulders the size of a small car, foreign to the stream, trucked in on tri axil flat beds from a distant quarry, are sitting next to the backhoe in a field above the stream. After extreme excavation by a backhoe, these massive stones move into place at the stream edge by means of a large claw arm crane attachment to the backhoe. Another backhoe with a twenty-four-inch bucket attachment excavates and rakes the stream bottom and edge clean and crisp to accept the stones.

The operator changes machinery and claw-handles the massive stones into place along the new bank edge established and verified by a consulting engineer using a transit and a laser. The stream, molded into a new form by the machines meets the consulting engineer's specifications for depth, width, and tilt. An inspector comes to approve the work, takes photos, authors a report then moves to the next job before returning to his office on Highway 421 in Trade, TN. A front-end loader reshapes the bank edge, first to get the machinery into the stream, then to mold and re-grade it to slope perfectly from the large adjoining field down to the huge well-placed stones. The cattle have moved away from the action and graze uphill occasionally watching the spectacle unfold. Then two workers sod and stake mesh for the entire sloped area preparing for plants and trees in the newly established riparian zone. The work begins every day at seven a.m. and ends at four p.m. when the operator leaves the site, and the heavy equipment stays in the stream until the next morning. The entirety of the work is based on calculations to reduce erosion, improve sediment transport, establish a riparian buffer, and assist in flood control.

Laurel Creek Low Water Level Summer
Pencil on Paper
Mark T. Wright

The backhoe and front-end loader, efficient in their work, can never feel the stream current; never feel the coolness of the water; never smell the earth; never know a salamander or damselfly nymph or snail or water snake or crawdad; never know how their extreme invasion of the stream effects life. The butterfly effect practiced. They never see the tread marks beneath the surface on the stream bottom, never know the suffering of the stream bottom beneath the weight of the machine, never know the rocks that they push down that took centuries to expose. The machines never feel the weight of a boulder or stone and never have the conversation asking where it wants to go. They tell them where they want them to go. Steel, hydraulics oil and power efficiently mold the new stream.

The operator sits above the stream, another job, another task, never touching a stone, a boulder, the water, or the earth. The steel claw and bucket are extensions of his hands and feet alien to the life in the stream. Joysticks, levers, pedals, gauges, hydraulic lines, diesel fuel and gears mingle in a magical syncopation to mold the earth and lift the massive stones into the specified spots outlined by the engineers and based on formulas executed repeatedly. Then at four o'clock, the operator leaves the stream for the night to go home away from the work and the stream. The machines sit, quietly, empty, imposing their weight in the stream marking where the work stopped for the day. They appear sad and abandoned, almost measuring the entire width of the stream, as a trickle of water runs around the treads timidly. They have gone from heated churning loud smoking diesel giants to cold still sleeping metal impositions sitting in haunting silence. The machines remain there in the stream until the next morning when the operator returns and work resumes.

There is no conversation with the stream, no partnering with nature, no accounting for specifics, and context and life. There is no room for trials and no time to revel in failures. The efficient and powerful machines cannot and have no intention of talking with the stream. They reject the conversation in lieu of commands from the engineer and the operator to complete the work as quickly and as dogmatically as possible. There is no need for conversation, no need for subtle attention, no need for time. They are deaf to the sound of the water. They are powerful and large, and there is only the task to complete efficiently and as planned, leaving a new stream form clean and perfect. There is no intimate lifelong stewardship.

This is undeniably an efficient machine at work, and we hope the cure is not worse than the symptoms. They execute the work to be final, expeditious, and succinct. However, there are no wet feet, cold hands, and smashed fingers from touching and moving rocks. There are no sore muscles, no contact with the water, no pressing against the earth, no watching the current before and as you change it, no checking for damage to the minnows, the salamanders, the crawdads, the mayflies. The machines never sweat water droplets into the stream from a forehead, becoming part of the water. There is no conversation with the stream or the children about their joy and responsibility to become future stewards, no example for them, no stories, no book, no adventure of the process, no sense of wonder. All they have seen is the pristine results without knowing the journey. Perhaps this is the best and only way to stabilize and save the stream to balance, if you did not live it every day and the best way to achieve the most impact for the money spent. To do nothing and remain asleep is the greater sin.

I take solace in the knowledge that the stream is a living life-giving entity that now and continually needs help, and as the crayfish, salamanders, nymphs, minnows, frogs, the water snake the children named Bobby, and water spiders draw life from her, so do I. The pain in my arms subsides and gives way to exhaustion and little satisfaction since I know that, as in archery, hitting and missing is the same thing, and as a sand painting all the work could be gone in a rain's moment. The hope is that nature will be kind and assist me in creating a revived and exuberant earth painting on a stream canvas. The hope is, even in the violence of a flood, that I have established and cultivated enough structure aiding the stream to resist damage and instead assist the water in being reborn and cultivated to enhance life.

The work involved redirecting the current, the stacking of boulders, the digging of drops and the creation of waterfalls. The restoration of the banks to help prevent erosion and limit the silt, is arduous and pushes this old man to the brink. But it has become a mission to bring her back to vibrant beauty and balance using the materials that are present in the stream and try to recreate an environment where delicate brook trout can flourish. Some may look upon this effort as a waste of time, an exercise in futility, a practice of self-indulgence. But in the end, it is practice and a making of something sustainable. A practice forgotten, or never experienced by so many. My son asked me, "Papa, what does a banker do?" I had to relegate my description to, "Nothing really." They make nothing, create nothing, discover nothing, heal nothing, touch nothing. This is not the exception in most professions. My own profession is not exempt; it has lost the concept of master builder and suffers from this plague of "non-doing;" the same ailment of detachment and delusion of creating without making.

Brookies are a trout that requires the purest water with rich oxygen, lower water temperature and more of a gravel bottom with less silt. They are delicate small fish. Having them here along with the salamanders, will be indicators of a successful healthy stream and verify the work. Years ago when I was stone sculpting birdbaths, my dearest friend said, "Those birdbaths are beautiful." I responded, "I am trying to elevate them to art, but if the birds don't like them, I have failed."

These small creatures were here inhabiting these waters at one time before the dawn of simpletons and before those who believe the stream is for their reckless rampage and pleasure, and before those who do not comprehend the religion of the water. I know the stream is a sacred thing, she is a sacred body on loan to us in this lifetime. We cannot own the water, but I do own the land containing the water and where she treads, and traverses, and I feel an intense and overwhelming commitment to protect her from those unwilling to acknowledge and respect her sacred existence. And so, with my melodrama and soap box in tow, I continue.

While contemplating the complexity of Laurel Creek,
I examined the water level, speed, depth,
and the curvature of the South bank.

Chapter IV

It rained one half inch yesterday. I was renewed watching the movement of the stream while listening to Mozart and then Kate Wolf. The sun was out for a brief period as it rained and I thought about what Nannie always said when it rained and, concurrently there was sun, "The devil is beatin' his wife." The same rain that temporarily traps me in the house forcing me to deal with domestic chores and allows me time to plan; that helps me calm my overzealous appetite to always be working outdoors; that makes me pause to reflect on the direct connection between rain and earth without feeling that the time thinking is wasted; that lures me to run naked under its caress on warm Appalachian days with the promise of rejuvenation and timeless youth screaming the name of Ponce de Leon of the mountains. That same rain that beats down a rhythm from the drum core of the sky gods on the roof, spilling rainwater into the gutters flowing as the stream; that brings out the smell of earth lingering in the air as some hypnotic erotic perfume; that oxygenates the Hansen's pond transforming the surface into overlapping explosive dimples; that enriches the tomato plants and the beans planted by the

Averys; that nourishes the grasses in the clearing, the ferns up the mountainside, the rhododendrons along the stream banks and roadside; the birches lining the stream edges, and the walnut trees scattered. That same rain that softens the sounds of the forest floor brittle from the dry July; that makes the leafy lichens celebrate a joyous dance of moisture with fluorescent green illumination on the darkened saturated bark as if the forest gods sprinkled light on the tree limbs; that renews the stream or contributes to its continued erosion.

This morning I watched a doe with fawn in tow trot across the mountain into and across the stream via the path that I had forged through the thickets. If I remain still, they will go about their business unaffected by my intrusion. Their eyesight is not particularly keen, but they are aware of any movement and sound that will spark a reaction. Over these last months I have seen many does and fawns, sometimes as many as six frolicking in the clearing and on the mountains side. Their brownish hollow hair allows them to blend into the woods flawlessly, only seen if they decide to move. Spooked, they jump, and bound away tail raised exposing an underbelly of stark white. Thus, the nickname "white tail deer." I had never seen the master of this domain, the male buck until last evening while driving the gravel road home from a visit to Boone. The sun had just dropped below the western tree line, so the entire scene was dimly lit, and the evening was still holding onto the last visages of light waiting for the night curtain to fall. One hundred yards from the house he came prancing down the mountain from behind the old tobacco barn across my path and stopped at the upper stream side edge of the road. He stood there majestic and unperturbed wearing an eight-point crown atop his head, thick necked, powerful and virile, high chest out. I knew he could not recognize me, but I had heard his grunts of dominance in the evenings and knew it was him.

I stopped the car when he passed in front of me. So, there we stopped, eye to eye; me in awe of this incredible animal and he acting as if he were posing for a *National Geographic* photo op. He looked at me through the window, calm and sure, nostrils flared, pupils dilated, grunting a word with me as he exhaled as if to introduce himself to a mere human commoner in the presence of royalty. It was a humorous reversal of the stereotype "deer in the headlights," because I was the animal paralyzed by his transcendent beams. The event lasted ten seconds, or five minutes, or twenty-five minutes; I don't know. Then he bowed his head slightly, marched slowly down the bank and trotted across the stream, then up the south side of the mountain. I finally saw the proud father of the many fawns—another moment of brilliance in the high country.

Yesterday I studied the soul of the current by locating the silt, sand and gravel deposits, small water flows and bottom scarring. I asked, "If I were a brookie, where would I be and what would I want?" What can I augment and understand, because the stream will change the idea on a whim of nature? She conversed with me about the things I could improve, and the areas that have been neglected for years left to fester in torment.

I saw a muskrat scurry across the property along the bank in the downstream direction. I spotted a den made of small twigs interwoven and lodged in the crevasse between a large boulder and the bank about two hundred yards downstream from the bridge. The entrance was hidden underwater next to the boulder. These rodents are mostly harmless but can be aggressive if cornered, and most people mistake them for a beaver. The smaller tail is the most obvious revealing feature in addition to the size. The beaver is much bigger. So, we all must be vigilant when the children come, to help them navigate clear of this unpredictable creature.

The stream showed me details of the degrading bank in micro detail and the areas where accruing heavy silt deposits hugged the bottom like small, peaked sand dunes at certain spots caused by soil run off and erosion. She showed me the piles of boulders accumulated from the last flood only a week ago, as if they were pebbles tossed from the hand of Atlas. I found other boulders holding steadfast in timeless determination, defying the extreme deluge and the hand of the giant, refusing to move—at least to the naked eye. Each proud and stubborn boulder realizes it weathered the last event, but the water will return to test each boulder's resolve repeating their timeless conversation. For now, I see them quiet and content to be resting and altering the slower recovering current. She showed me that the water moving around my legs magically, affected by rain a mile away, five hundred feet away, fifty feet away, could have happened hours or even minutes ago upstream. My simple presence in the stream temporarily alters the current downstream. Every action has an impact. So, I am constantly vigilant of my actions. The butterfly effect is real and is blatantly obvious in this stream.

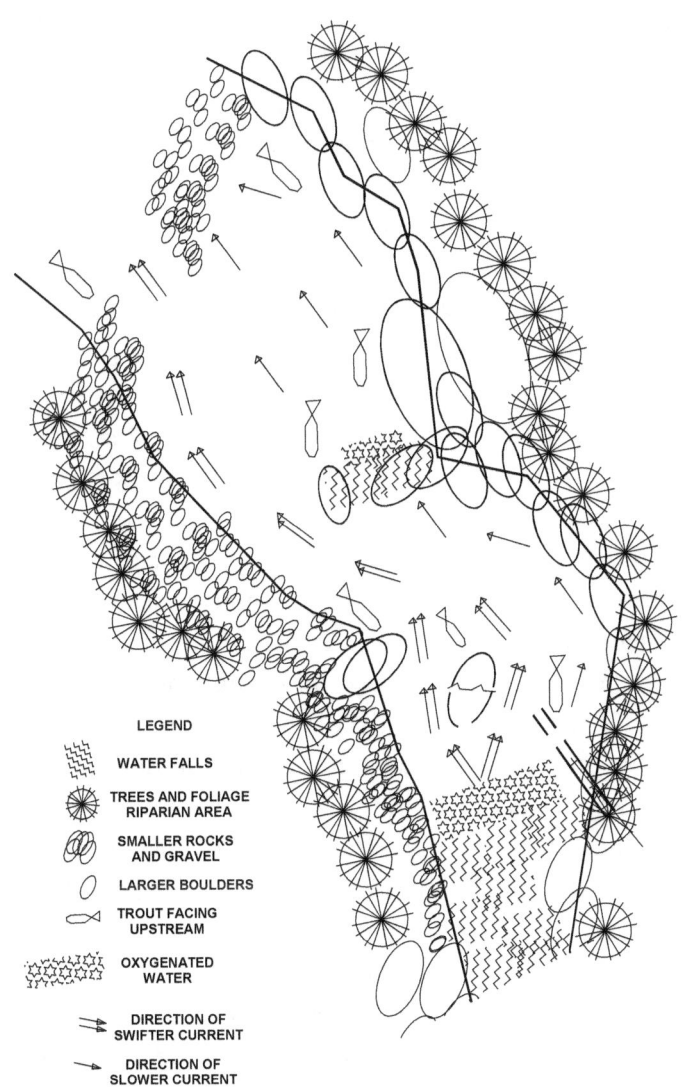

LEGEND

WATER FALLS

TREES AND FOLIAGE
RIPARIAN AREA

SMALLER ROCKS
AND GRAVEL

LARGER BOULDERS

TROUT FACING
UPSTREAM

OXYGENATED
WATER

DIRECTION OF
SWIFTER CURRENT

DIRECTION OF
SLOWER CURRENT

HEALTHY STREAM STUDY MODEL

Time has molded her. I now become another entity, the neophyte in nature's arena, a blank canvas; a stumbling piece of malleable clay; a piece of raw steel hammered into an infinite layered Damascus blank by these healing waters. My actions are intended to help the stream wash out the silt; curtail the erosion of the banks; carve out the main channels; become centered and rich and to establish deep holes beneath waterfalls. My actions are to disperse its energy during floods instead of concentrating its destructive force; to oxygenate and enrich water life; to polish rock and expose new boulders asleep under years of debris and lifetimes; to create new homes for small creatures; to be cyclical in its washout of debris, and to work for the good of the stream. This is an objective conversation practiced with the stream. It is only one facet of a complex relationship. When in these waters, know that reverence practiced, yields priceless moments. I want to leave it for my children to continue the work and maintenance as stewards of this land and planet.

It is amazing that this delicate gentle creature today, soothing in her serenity, can tomorrow transform into a roaring vibrating tumult of churning brown foaming water by a heavy rain. The water exists in extremes and can assist in the stream's revival or choose to punish it with excessive force. It can caress the stream, or violently carve and steal the wealth of soil at the bank edges as it rolls by. I must believe that the water is unaware of the harm that it often inflicts on the stream environment. I must believe that the water has only good intentions and wishes to partner with me and the stream to enhance its life and not harm it. We must forgive the water's indiscretion and act biblically and forgive it for it knowing not what it does, because we as humans have recklessly interposed ourselves into the stream environment, between rain, water and stream and influencing its decisions and contributing to its extremes. In that light, I work the stream by redirecting and clearing the stream channel in hopes to coerce the water to adjust and work for us, and not against us in this unique environment.

Today I am working the stream before the rain comes again. My hands stiff from the continuous partnering with a shovel and pick handle, have developed small hitches of the tendons in the fingers of both hands. But I cannot resist the draw and the mission of being in the water. Hopefully, the rain will stop me, and I can work in the house. But every precious moment draws me to the water and its needs. The stream life seems to have begun to return, or that is my illusion. However, life does seem to be moving in the clearer flowing water freed from silt and taking up residence in varied depths and with places for the smallest of creatures to thrive.

I am listening to Jimmy Reed's *Big Boss Man* and Freddie King's *I'm Tore Down* while doing this work, and something seems absolutely correct about it. Sacrilegious, but the work is difficult and dancing in the stream to James Brown and Don Covey relieves the pain. I do believe the neighbors question my sanity, but they do not question my tenacity and draw entertainment from my perceived follies. There is a stark limitation on the scope of work I can accomplish since I'm confined to the existing stream bed and banks. There are endless solutions within these confines but few the stream and water desire.

There is joy in a simple act of doing, of primal work, of physical labor, of sculpting the land, of making something, of helping, of standing back and bearing witness to work done,

51

or to work in progress. There is simple pleasure in the practice, with pure intention to aid and repair, of gently leaving a physical mark on the earth's face attempting to eradicate the scars slashed by the switchblade apathy of generations that came before me, whether intentional or not. There is a satisfaction to execute a plan that is praying to aid the stream to enhance life. There is a mesmerizing wonder of touching every stone, every boulder, feeling the heaviness that gravity inserts into every object and the smoothness that they possess from years of the rubbing water. There is a brilliance of the cool water enveloping my feet and hands lowering my temperature like soothing chamber music and isolating me from the heat of the day's events.

The real test will be soon if the water temperature can maintain at sixty-five degrees Fahrenheit, while the air temperature continues to rise. The stream will function as the judge, and the brookies, salamanders and mayfly nymphs are the jury.

Each day in the water ends at sundown with a reflection on the work completed and a question posed to the stream, "Is the work, ok?" I always receive my answer over the next few days and always carried on the back of the next rain. I gather the tools, wet and much heavier than they were this morning. I take my leave walking the path I have created up the bank, carrying the stream and water up the mountain with me. My hip waders, boots, trousers, shirt, and gloves are saturated and embraced by the water, as are my emotions and psyche. My boots squish, squish, squish pumping in air and water out as I walk to the small shed to deposit my pick and shovel for the night. I open the small door and toss them in, hearing them hit the floor with a steel clang marking the end of the workday like an awkward muted dinner bell.

Riffles Near the Bridge
Photograph by Todd Bush

I make the sixty-foot climb up the mountain to the house, wet and tired. I pass the trees covered with lichens which illuminate to a fluorescent green during rain. They are amazing life forms, expressing an incredible symbiotic partnership between fungus and algae. They are small leaflike mosses clinging to the trees causing no damage and asking only that they are given a structure to stay and hold while living. The fungus provides the structure for the algae to live and in return the algae feed the fungus. Since they derive their nutrients from the moist air, they are a barometer of good air quality, and they are covering the trees in abundance. As I make the climb, my pulse accelerates and I become aware of my heart and lungs, and I am grateful to breathe this precious dense mountain air. Once up to the south facing porch, I survey the day's work then I sit in the plastic lounge chair, remove my boots and waders. I wedge the boots between the porch rail balusters, heels down toes up open facing south to dry overnight. I hang the waders from old plant hooks set into the porch beams on the west side to air dry. The boots and waders dry by mountain air evaporating the water to the atmosphere riding the breezes to hitchhike that mystical cycle of the water.

The water has caused the skin on my fingers to shrivel from the daylong exposure in the stream, spots scatter over the lenses of my glasses from splashes, my trousers, shirt, and other clothes soaked through hang inside on the iron stair rail to dry. These wet items, welcomed by the house, unite the stream, water, and house in an intimate relationship of evaporation. I am wearing and carrying the stream to meet the heart of the house. Every evening, either sheer exhaustion, or fleeting sunlight forces me to stop work. I shower off any harmful elements hidden on my skin by the conduit of the stream water. Although clean and clear and supporting life, I am cautious of lurking parasites and bacteria harmful to humans. The water from the well flows through the shower, over me and flushes down through the septic system into the leach field pipes, then filtered by the land flows back to the stream. I have stopped but the stream continues.

8-18-21

Yesterday I worked for eight hours reconstructing the small waterfall fifty feet west and upstream from the bridge. The weather is beautiful, pleasant, and sunny, especially for an August day. The vertical drop at the falls is too severe to navigate easily for small fish, and I made efforts to graduate and step the flow, opening a wide channel so it better communicates gently with the upper stream. This strategy will repeat at locations where there are severe vertical drops, to allow trout to navigate downstream and upstream. If executed properly, it becomes a "highway of less effort" created for trout to swim against the current without having to jump the falls upstream. This is not complete, as the work must be incremental, and requires patience while I ask the stream for help. I plan, I listen, then I execute a short term and a long-term plan that I hope the stream helps me achieve.

I was working intently in the water and entranced by the movement and sound of the falls, when I looked up and saw a tall, thin slightly pot-bellied grey-haired man in a ball cap and waders leaning on the rail on the bridge above me.

"Hey, I'm Al, I heard the shovel banging but didn't see anyone. I live just up the road, first road on the right past the Hansens house up the hill straight on up to the top."

He was wearing a dark blue Simms fleece pullover under his grey waders and a pair of brown worn leather wading boots that looked as old as the bridge. Behind him was a dark blue '05 Ford F-150 pickup truck, open back with a steel tool chest mounted across the bed at the cab and with three fly rods sticking above the sides of the bed.

"I live in Charlotte but built a house up the road…down here. I guess really up here," he chuckled. "My wife and I come here to be in the mountains when the weather is nice, and I can fly fish. What are you doing there?"

I walked closer to him under the bridge so I could hear better, still in the water, I had to yell over the sound of the falls so he could hear me. "I just moved here from Macon, Georgia, and I am working on the stream." Seeing he was a fisherman but not yet knowing if he was an angler, I proceeded with cautious slight pomposity (as all fly fishermen have the humorous tendency to do), since we believe the low life of fishing is bait fishing, and of course we argue that flyfishing is of royal stature. Even though most of us began our fishing lives with a Zebco 33 closed face spinning reel and heavy fiberglass rod, a worm or doughballs, and a bobber, we tend to dismiss that as naïve past, and speak as if we have been exclusively fly fishing since we were able to hold a rod in hand, and even pre-birth. So, we all proceed in conversations, speaking foreign specialized jargon, about fishing, line and rod weight, leader and tippet size, nymphs, streamers, and dry flies, as if we are members of the royal court of fly fishing, and those who are not receive our gracious heartfelt sympathy.

"To make it flow again, deep enough and strong enough maybe to support brookies," I responded.

"A lot of work. I just got done over at Beaver Creek and caught ten in this one deep hole in half the day."

"What were they?"

"Mostly rainbows but a few browns, ten to twelve inches. Nice day."

"I'll say, nice day! Where were you fishing again?"

"Beaver Creek."

"I don't know that place. I've been busy working on the stream, steps and house and trying to get the cottage started and haven't had a chance to explore. Just places around Blowing Rock and down at the Watauga."

"When I come back, I'll take you sometime. Are you here full time and what do you do? I'm a retired electrical engineer from Duke Energy."

"I'm an architect but I won't hold being an engineer against you, and yes, I am here full time. My kids are in Kentucky, and I am here."

"The stream looks good."

"Thanks, think it will hold fish?"

"Looks like it."

"I saw a twelve-inch rainbow dart downstream while I was working today. What were you using earlier when you were fishing?"

"I was euro-nymphing with a single black and white heavy nymph with a red-hot spot and no indicator."

"Never tried that but did real well last February with a double nymph rig with an olive-colored gold head plain nymph I tied like a large zebra nymph, and a flashback pheasant tail dropper and indicator down at the Watauga. And did pretty well, believe it or not, with a large cinnamon colored dry fly elk hair caddis and a zebra dropper at Helton."

"Never been there, always wanted to go but isn't it about an hour north just short of Virginia?"

"Yep, but it is so beautiful. A bit crowded at the lower section, but the upper section near the old Helton school has less pressure. Last year I went in the lower section and there was an angler about every one hundred yards of the entire stream for a couple miles. So, I went upstream down from the school, right across from the old church and did well. By the way, I have an extra shovel if you have nothing to do. I even have a left-handed shovel if you need it."

"Well, thanks for the offer but I have a few things to do before I head back. I need to clean up a tree that fell before I leave tomorrow. But I come back in a few weeks, and I'll show you a few spots around here and maybe we can hit Helton."

"Absolutely, I need to find some new spots to take the children when they come down and I need an excuse to stop working for a day. Looking forward to it. Here's my number. Thanks for stopping by and be safe heading back to Charlotte."

"Will do, see ya."

"Thanks, see ya." He is an angler and has a reverence for the water. Now back to work.

View of the bridge and Laurel Creek looking down mountain.
Pencil, pen and ink on paper
Mark T. Wright

The first step in the work involves eliminating dead water areas where no current exists. This is obvious peering down through clear water discovering the areas with sedimentary deposits on the bottom, and if we drop a leaf boat in the water in these areas it does not move downstream but drifts aimlessly, usually in circles and usually along the bank edges. Executing the simple idea of displacement, I moved unwedged larger boulders kicked and carried by the cascading water from their randomly tumbled positions to the areas of dead water. I dug other stubborn rocks and boulders from the center bottom, stacking them into these dead spots until they reached the surface redirecting the current. This raises the water level in the stream while narrowing and concentrating water to a center channel. The second step is to eliminate the many rock damns and make the falls simple meandering and step with a continuous channel combined with the cascade down to the bottom to the falls to the deep hole. Whether these dam impediments are manmade (my supposition) or not, they cause restricted flow and often stagnant pools in the dry summer.

As part of this effort, repair of the area surrounding the concrete structure supporting the north section of the bridge due to erosion was essential. Earlier this year I had delivered twenty tons of rip rap stone to help restructure a drainage ditch from the gravel road west and downstream of the bridge to filter runoff and reduce silt into the stream and shore up the area under the bridge adjacent to the bridge pier. I moved eight tons of stone across the bridge, depositing the pieces under the bridge, against the bridge structure, and out into the water. This too helped displace water and focus the current back to the middle channel and away from the bridge pier, reducing scouring and silt deposits.

This work creates a sloped channel in a meandering pattern of faster current slithering around rocks and drops oxygenating the water as it cascades. One rock in the main channel helps break the current's acceleration because of the drop across the gravel bottom. I will leave this area to its own means for a brief time hoping that nature assists me in carving out a deeper run. Once established, I will expand and bend the channel width, which will spread out the impact of the faster current over a greater surface area and lighten the flow so trout can swim upstream easier. I will revisit this, checking on my assistant's progress.

I sat my shovel down in the stream while I moved the larger boulders. After I completed this work, I retrieved my shovel by the top of the wooden handle, blade in stream. "Damnation crap!" In a New York second the current, swift and shifty at that area, unexpectedly grabbed the flat steel blade forcing it downstream like a sharp-edged pendulum crashing into my leg causing a two inch wide cut on my shinbone. I was wet, wading in only boots and shorts, so the blade made a clean unencumbered slice into my skin. As the blood began to flow and run down my shin, it was washed by the moving cool waters, dulling the pain, as if to say, "I just made you look but now I'll relieve the pain a bit." The cool water washed around and across the bruised cut, soothing while washing the blood downstream. Bright red at the cut, it mixed quickly looking like floating light candle smoke, merging with the water, and dissipating downstream. Maybe this was the moment that I became blood brothers with the stream, water, rocks and stone, as a secondary outcome to my carelessness.

This was a painful lesson on the forces at work in this arena, and practice for me to understand how the water and the stream control and interact with objects introduced to this stage. At another section of the stream where the stream is wider and the current slows, this would not have happened. But at this location in the stream where banks choke down, the fall is more severe, the current accelerates and enriches the water with oxygen, and exerts and concentrates its surprising power. This was a wakeup call telegraphed in stream and water language, and it was the stream emphasizing her seemingly innocent and hidden unpredictability, force, and control.

Harry and I moving boulders.

Chapter V

8-26-21

I spent hours selecting and excavating boulders to move, developing a center channel, creating deeper runs, and then depositing the stones along the stream side into the waiting fingers of the birches, where the soil was eroding. The lack of a center channel, caused initially by excessive sediment transport, continually adds to the sediment deposits, and encourages erosion and unstable streambanks. I am trying to stabilize the banks continuously and consistently with stones as I go along as base for re-establishing a rich riparian zone with soil and native plant life. This may be a lifelong effort as nature will help me most of the time, but then will destroy the work other times. The goal is to reach an equilibrium between the ideal and the natural.

I use boulders and stones dug and wrenched from the stream bed, relocating them to create a deeper stream bottom, depositing them to create the new stream edge and meandering shape with a bank sloping up from the water to the soil. So, I am deepening the stream at the same time raising the bank, hoping that I do not run out of material to reconstruct the bank edges. The material has always been here in one condition or another, and I believe the original stream channel was filled in and washed back into the humped center bottom of the current stream bed along with boulders carried from upstream. I am simply listening to the voice of the water and in partnership with the stream exposing the stream channel that is here under debris.

Half of the new edges I have created are of a lower degree of slope rising gently upwards from the water meeting the old edge of the violated soil at the top. This allows a moderate controlled overflow of the stream when seasonal and severe flooding occurs and lightens the impact of the deluge on the unsuspecting soil by spreading out and dispersing the damaging energy over a wider stone and riparian plant covered area. Other spots require steeper slopes, near the roadside section of the stream, to reduce edge incision, undercutting and bank erosion and help redirect water flow. And still other spots require steep slopes, acting as temporary formwork while I deliberately coax the stream to make new edges and new routes creating a sustained center channel. Later I will taper these steep slopes more gently from land to water. Later I plan to place topsoil over the upper sections of the bank, over sand, over stone meeting the current edge of the soil and plant grasses, evergreen azaleas, and rhododendrons for reestablishing the riparian area. Still other spots require deflectors and cross veins in addition to the newly constructed meandering edges to help redirect and concentrate the current to the center of the stream. These structural tools help raise the water level of the stream on restricted areas in addition to funneling water helping to recreate and maintain a center channel.

Additional tools in the stream adjusting arsenal are simple stone structures called deflectors and cross deflectors. The deflectors, in general, are single arms of stone extending from one side of the bank into the stream close to the center angled slightly upstream. They are thicker in width at the bank edge tapering to single front stones as they move toward the center of the stream. These are three dimensional objects and as they move from the single lowest stones in the front center of the stream, they also slope slightly upward to meet the bank level making a gentle concave shape. The lowest level stone is even with the lowest water flow and when the stream swells the water level moves up over higher stone incrementally helping focus water to the center channel. They are not dams and instead direct water away from the stream banks while gaps in the front rocks allow faster water to flow through while also helping stabilize the banks. Cross veins are two deflectors placed in a V pattern with the point of the V facing upstream and the structure spans from bank to bank. A cross vein is a deflector mirrored around the center of the stream channel.

It is difficult to achieve balance between the proper massing of stones, the height, the proper opening locations and size of stones, the proper angle and taper of the stones, and rise to the bank, and the water flow in every stream condition with every rainfall accumulation. It is best to attempt these when the stream is at a lower level since each stone displaces water, raises the water level, and increases the current speed. Patience is paramount and each structure requires its own fine tuning during low water and after a hard rain. I have found I cannot build these strong enough or massive enough, with the perfect combination of slope and stones in every condition to anticipate and accommodate every event. Nature and the stream unequivocally have the last laugh and I repair and tune the structures the best I can as continuous maintenance. They morph into hybrid structures from the perfect theoretical form molded and modified by me and the stream, eventually evolving to forms, which will be absorbed into the stream family.

It is, as a friend described to me, a twist on the childhood game of "tug-of-war" where the original goal is to defeat the other team by pulling them in one direction. A flag tied on the rope, dead center, pulled in opposition by each team past a certain spot declares a winner. The new game is one of balance. Where the opposing sides line up and tug, and when one side is winning, the strongest member of the other team switches sides to equal out the tug and find an equilibrium. The goal is to maintain the flag dead center. As each team tires and continues to pull, the exchange of members may vary but the goal is to intuitively find the balance between numbers and members as the conditions change. It is a physical act of subordinating one's ego to balance.

I'm reminded of La Cité Frugès, the workers houses designed in Pessac, France by the iconic architect Le Corbusier in 1924. They are now listed as a UNESCO World Heritage Site. These houses were initially a quintessential example of modern "affordable" architecture: white, stoic, flat roofed, ribbon windows, pure forms devoid of decoration. Forty years after they were initially constructed, as these were lived in, changing hands, and becoming privately owned; needs over time led to a natural evolution and modifications or demolition. One owner added a pitched roof over certain areas, narrowed windows to add wall space, enclosed spaces under the second floor for extra space, among others. Some in the profession say there was a conflict between the architecture and living, and a failure of the design, or it was sacrilege to touch the work of the master, but I believe those reactions to be farthest from the truth and, it was a show of the genius of Le Corbusier. This home evolved naturally from its initial design and modified has lived on. Yes, changed. And we can pompously debate the aesthetic modifications into perpetuity from an academic and professional point of view. But this house lives on breathing in and out.

I have about thirty percent of the lower east stream started, but there is a huge amount of work there. Every moved stone, every worked bank, every step in the stream has an unmistakable and immediate butterfly effect on the rest of the stream, and I must be careful and wary of all effects. I am an architect, and it seems appropriate to do this. Stream design is a patient search, and as Eeyore from *Winnie the Pooh* said, "Brains first, and then hard work." That is the way to build a stream. I know it seems easy, but not everyone can do it.

Reflecting in quiet repose with vigilant study of the stream workings is paramount. It is as critical as moving boulders into place and as essential as listening. The work is a fluid ever changing process. I wait patiently, wonder and when I hear her whisper the clues, and after deliberation from the study, generate design ideas and experiments from the perspective of multiple and diverse entities. After I see the clues, refine a design idea, only then do I execute the back breaking demanding work!

I have moved most boulders straight backed, bent-kneed, breath in, exhaled on the effort, lifted erect with slightly bent arms pulling the stone close to my waist. Resting them on my belt and pelvis, treading carefully on the remaining slick rocks, I walk them carefully to their new location. My years of Qigong, as well as my Irish genes, have paid off in practice. I cannot help but conjure images of my ancestors working Irish fields moving stones to plant potatoes. Irony repeated. I laughed to myself remembering my favorite Irish joke: Two Irishmen have come to New York on holiday. So excited, they walk by a bar. That is the joke.

The difficulty, other than the size and shape, and the effort to dislodge the boulder from its suction hold in the stream bottom with a shovel or pry bar, is finding the "handles" that allow a grip on the underside of the boulder where slick algae has not yet permeated the stone, and where friction is my friend. Otherwise, gripping the boulder becomes precarious, the rock may slip and twist from your grip sending the stone from your hands to an unwanted doom marked by a massive splash. At that moment, when this happens, I make an immediate and urgent plea to the rock gods that the crashing boulder misses all my appendages. Then a stop, and a pensive check to see if my prayers are answered before resuming the work.

Boulders I cannot yet move scream for attention, but I must ask them to pipe down, be patient and I will get there. Often, they will only partially push their face above the veil of the stream bottom, as if they are watching the work progress waiting to decide if it is acceptable before exposing any more of their surface, slightly surveying the terrain hiding the tremendous body below. Others hide until the newly developed current or next flood exposes them, while still others are brilliant, moved by the hand of nature. These occupy the stream permanently and converse with the stream under all conditions.

Every rock, every stone, every piece of gravel, every particle of sand I move by hand, but only where it wants to go. There is a place where each rock should be and they let me know, fickle as they are, happy in one spot for a while then leaving, shifting, moving, falling, tumbling, and settling in a completely different spot after the next rain. I have done my best to unclog every vein and allow life to flow freely in her. I have been cautious and humble and tread lightly because there is life existing on the underbelly and between these stones. And as I have progressed with the work on the stream, I witness new life emerge, more life accumulating and returning, or dropped from the gods as the stream holds the water consistently swifter and more oxygenated.

After months of working the stream, and during a visit by the children, Harry and I explored the water beginning at the Watauga River and the confluence of the stream, up and over the waterfall to the house by hiking the entire stream until reaching the area around the bridge. Harry and I turned over rocks, searching the underbellies of each stone, and we were excited to find numerous reddish brown and olive northern dusky salamanders between two and three-inches long slithering elegantly away for other cover. These delicate tiny amphibious creatures, with hind limbs longer than their front legs, are nocturnal with a small range (just a few yards) to forage, and they will eat anything and can regenerate limbs. Their life cycle is like frogs beginning as eggs laid under water, growing to larvae, and developing gills, then the larvae sprout front limbs, then hind limbs, then magically metamorphosis occurs, and the time comes for it to move to moist land. The salamander will not venture far from the water because it must return to the water to mate and lay eggs in spring and start the cycle over.

Being amphibians, they are cold blooded so in winter brumation begins at the whim of nature as they cannot control their metabolic rate. Brumation, taken from Latin for winter solstice, is an involuntary state of torpor when the surrounding air and water temperature falls. Some salamanders beef up for the winter and store food in their tail and bury themselves in underground burrows of other animals since they cannot dig themselves, or in deep rock crevasses, or they bury themselves in the mud to stay warm and safe. They need water to survive, water rich in oxygen and which will not freeze all the way to the bottom of the stream. Then when the temperature warms, they become active since their metabolic rate increases. They can only generally brumate for three to four months without dying. Sizzling summer temperatures also cause problems for these fragile creatures. Estivation is a way they slow down, seek shade and cooler water to help them cope with the hot temperatures. Seeing them here now in the stream after the work, is a gift from the stream gods and a small testament that what I am doing is aiding the survival of these beautiful creatures, at least in my section of the planet.

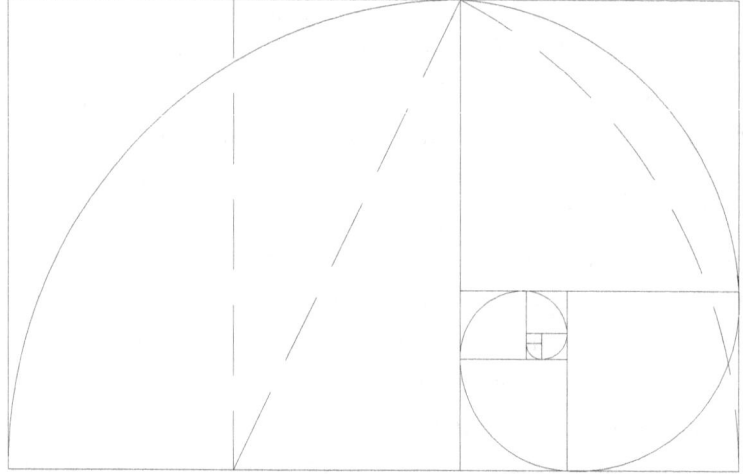

Golden mean

The next few rocks Harry turned over yielded more treasures and gave me an excuse later in the evening to explain the golden mean and the Fibonacci sequence occurring in real time. He found tiny freshwater black colored snails no bigger than one eighth of an inch in diameter clinging to the bottom of the rocks. I was reminded of the story when the snail met a centipede. The snail asked the centipede, "How do you make those hundreds of feet move, I only have one?" The centipede tried to answer but when he had to try to think about it, he was frozen and could not move. So, for now, mathematical and geometric connections took a back seat to the simple magic of nature; to the wonderful adventure and innocent open exploration in the water. These small mollusks are gastropods since they have a singular muscular foot for movement. Their singular spiral shell, soft at the beginning then hardening as it grows from the center spiral, is the quintessential nautilus shape at a microscopic scale. We found at least three to four of these algae eaters scraping food from the under surface of rocks with each large stone we turned over. These aquatic snails are primarily nocturnal creatures, and as their friends the salamander, require fresh water that provides them with the food source they need to survive.

Still other rocks yielded the nymphs that later will become damselflies, dragonflies, blue wing olives, and pale morning duns, and march browns. They have streamlined flattened bodies as they cling to the rock bottoms allowing the rushing water to flow over them with little resistance. Having an exoskeleton, the insect grows inside but the skeleton does not, and this outer skin sheds occasionally through its life span. As they grow, they develop critical things such as hidden wings for the next magic. Finally, their last aquatic act, the skeleton splits one last time and a newly hatched winged insect emerges, either in the water or on its surface then quickly flies to a nearby tree or bush to rest and dry its wings. While working in the stream I am constantly visited by what I think to be the same single damselfly buzzing close to me, and I know she was once a nymph beneath a rock.

As we continued our adventure, the water became so clear we could see the bottom without intrusion. As we move rocks, we see small explosions of silt and a blur scurry across the stream bed. When it stops, a few inches away we see a backward moving greenish brown crayfish looking at us through the water. Poised to defend, as we have disturbed him and now his back hair is up, he sets with claws (two of his ten legs) ready. This small crustacean is a predator, a scavenger, and prey in this stream environment. These amusing creatures walk forward and swim backwards. They swim by beating pairs of paddles called swimmerets on each body segment, but when startled they drive a fast tail flip and propel themselves backwards in quick jerks. They eat anything and are mostly nocturnal. They are vulnerable after molting when they shed their exoskeleton, exposing a soft exterior until the outer shell hardens. They have gills but can also breathe air and can live outside water for days. These tiny builders also excavate deep holes next to the stream, leaving ziggurat-like chimney mounds of mud at the entrance they pushed out as if they are building small temples to the moon god Nanna. We see these scattered along the stream edge. As a general measure of stream quality, the more crawdads we find the healthier the water. Since over sedimentation, damns and erosion destroys their habitat my work of eliminating these obstacles appears to coincide with the abundance of crawdads returning. I did not see them when I started work.

Years ago, in Kentucky, a manufacturing facility burned dumping chemicals into a small stream. The amounts were not enough to kill the smallmouth bass and bream population in the stream, but the chemicals migrated miles downstream.

However, the amounts killed the frogs, crawdads and freshwater snails living in the stream. Since the chemicals eliminated the food source for the fish, the fish died or migrated elsewhere further upstream, leaving a dead section of water for years. This did not kill the entire stream ecosystem and it recovered after a twenty-five-year fish barren existence. The takeaway is that the smallest most delicate organisms are the "canary in the coal mine" and that these small creatures warn us of impending problems long before we are fully aware.

I always ask for help from the water and stream and often I receive it, but she is reluctant and very fussy. However, success comes only with fearless effort and the ability to laugh at failures. And there is no writing unless there is work. There is nothing to say unless there is the doing, and there is no sense in doing unless striving to do well. But she knows that I have proven my intentions, and she is breathing easier with a cautious trust and with more clarity from my efforts. The trout new to the stream might never know the effort, unless they hear the story from the salamanders and the larger older crayfish. The returning flora may save the memory in their roots. The insects will only know the work that happens outside the confines of winter. The water may forget, but the stream remembers.

The water is continuous, alive, fluid, ever changing and connected by a relay race of molecular energy held and guided in a beautiful partnership by the negative confined space of the stream. Someday, it is possible that the same water that meanderingly flows here now, over and around my feet, through my hands, over stream belly, rock, and boulder, will solemnly and systematically make its way back, flowing down this stream after making its miraculous planetary circular journey, and may remember what we did together. That returning water may not recognize its partner completely because by that time other water will have made the journey its own, and the stream will have worked with quiet grace and violent torrent to shape an ever-evolving form.

Margaret Annie directing the action while Harry and I toil away moving sediment.

Chapter VI

The viburnum, oatgrass, and small ferns are as "thick as thieves" and are as strong as they will be this season hitting the pinnacle of their yearly life cycle arch. Standing six feet tall in spots they line the banks as a not so imposing barrier along each side of the stream. I have worn a path just wide enough for one person to walk through this brush from my frequent steps to the stream. My footsteps have stamped down the soil compressing it with repetition so that no weeds can penetrate. It is now a path that the deer use every morning on their way to cross the stream. I am the animal that made this new path that other animals share. Although our movements have a much different purpose, they come from the open clearing, funnel down and compress with this path, and then disperse at the stream. Their footprints overlap mine, which overlaps theirs as we make the same track down the mountain across the green through the thickets and briars to the stream. The animal residents of these mountains mimic my deliberate, almost daily journey, as I mimic theirs.

The children came for four days, and time stops with unspeakable delight as I clip the "wings from every minute" when I see them. Fall is coming, and the first leaves are reluctantly dropping and transforming into leaf boats drifting downstream. I watch them closely to see what currents and eddies and riffles have developed to assist them on their journey. They begin filling the high-country ridge lines as if on fire with the energy of a Cézanne painting. Brilliant melodic patches of yellow, browns and burning reds are the prevalent colors hugging the deciduous trees interspersed brilliantly among the mountain's flagship evergreen trees. The mystical magical floating falling shapes are varied, making up the spectacular armada that falls from the sky joining the other ships. No sails, no motors, no oars, just the stream and her laughter tumble and power the drifting tiny vessels. My son tells me the number of passengers on each boat depending on the size of the leaf and as it drifts gently, he describes the interaction of the crew. Then the leaf would hit turbulence and drops, and eddies, and rocks, and he would tell of the gallant efforts of the crew to save the ship from peril. Then he would let me know if there were survivors and which passengers were alive to float to the next section.

I worked in an area immediately downstream from the bridge while my son was playing nearby on the bank. There is a huge amount of sediment in this area, much to my chagrin but to the delight of my son. I pushed the shovel easily into this matter unlike the stone stream bottom. There is at least three feet of sand deposited in a three foot by ten-foot area. Better sand than silt, but still an area in need of correction. As I begin to lift the shovel, still below the water surface, the sand intersperses with the water bleeding over the sides of the shovel blade creating a ghostly underwater haboob of minute dispersed particles and releasing microscopic plants and animals. The tiny fragments of sand, organic matter, and microscopic marine life suspend in the water for a moment then fall into chaotic formation funneled downstream by the current.

Heavy at the beginning but losing weight as the water drains and the shovel breaks the surface, I lift the mixture from the stream and deposit it high on the bank. When I do this work a congregation of small minnows gathers immediately downstream behind the shovel oblivious to me, and ready to worship at the church stream of the uncovered micro critters. The faithful gather facing upstream to pick out their meal from the hazy water until the stream clears and the service restarts with my next shovel. I create a dust storm, but I cannot stop the stream from clearing the water, watching the particles float away fluidly, quietly wrapping around my ankles. Many think this is our reality: impotent and insignificant in the grand scheme of things, and that we are only a small particle that can be swept away downstream. The beauty you realize, from working in the water, is that we inevitably travel downstream, but may all the while experience one hell of a trip in the process. Each small insignificant particle plays a role in carving a center channel, smoothing stones and boulders and carrying mystical life along its journey. We should not presume to know which ones are critical—they all are.

I shoveled the sand from the bottom area near the bridge and packed the bank with sand creating a small beach for my son. He made sandcastles on the bank and rock islands with walls as a mighty fortress rivaling Troy, to keep out the zombies. There were precise numbers of inhabitants in the castle and adjoining village enjoying their safe harbor and leading specific lives. But the building broke abruptly when there came rock bombs from the blond curly headed giant, tossed into the air hitting the stream with an explosive bump and mushroom action like a cannonball. The excitement of the assault grew to a frenzy of attacks as the giant took hands full of sand and sprayed the entire scene with hundreds of projectiles hitting the water with a shotgun scattered effect, as opposed to the massive cannonball.

As I shook off the sand from my clothes and hat, I turned, and I saw a small head with beautiful curly blond hair and magnificent blue eyes tilt up and look at me and I heard a tiny voice say, "Sorry, Papa." I tossed the shovel to the bank and my work immediately stopped. Then joyously we grabbed handfuls of sand and rocks, leaves, and sticks and together we joined the battle. As I sent stick after stick and leaf boat after leaf boat filled with zombie invaders downstream to launch an attack on his castles, he defended them vigorously. As the best general, he prepared his defense and launched his offensive attack defeating his foes with pebble bombs sending my armada limping downstream.

So, I grabbed a hand full of sand and helped him with his explosions and assault on the villagers and the castle. I took my shovel and dug more sand for his fortress. He was very particular as to where to place each deposit of sand as a master-builder running his project, and as particular as I when placing each stone. He knows about the stream and the brookies, and the rainbows and the salamanders, and the nymphs and the snails. He has caught them all, held them all, examined them all gently and respectfully as an intent archeologist, yelled with delight after each discovery, absorbed the knowledge of each life, understands the fragility of this ecosystem, spoken to his teddy about their sentient existence, explained the experiences to others, and thanked them all and let them go.

Later he and Margaret Annie ventured upstream barefooted in the water, on their day's expedition looking for the water snake they named Bobby and whatever other discoveries happened in their path. Harry said if it is alive, it needs a name. The day was warm, the water clear, the sun was gracing the stream with dappled light through the birches, and the stream welcomed their footsteps. I waited at the bridge watching them explore on their own and walk through the middle of the stream gingerly feeling every bottom stone with their feet. As they moved away from me, upstream, their image began to merge with the magic of the stream fading into fragments of light becoming part of the reflections held on the water's surface. The sound of their voices and small splashes began to blend with the voice of the stream until vanishing into the melody of cascading water. The water that first touches them, seconds later moves elegantly downstream over rocks and stream bed, over years of living and buried invisible footprints, embraces me but never stops, then moves further downstream to touch other lives. As Mclean said, "Eventually all things merge into one." They walked as far as I could still see them together, siblings, innocent unassuming kindred spirits, and it occurred to me in real time where I was in the stream and my place in this universe. These two beautiful souls, the woods fairy and old man began their journey far upstream from me in time on this planet. My time here is downstream from these wondrous beings, but we have now merged into one, and I have the gift of being able to recognize this.

When I was upstream in their shoes, my father abandoned my mother and my younger brother and sister. He left when I was four years old. Luckily, we moved in with my great grandparents and grandparents since my mother worked full time at the local tobacco corporation headquarters. Years later after a series of unfortunate events, and after we moved to suburbia, I was working my first job at fourteen and worried about my mother's drug addiction, paying rent, and how we were going to eat. Poverty was my upstream location when I was Margaret Annie's age, and it serves me well sometimes to remember and look upstream miles past my children, and use it as a benchmark, to measure from where I have come. Now these two have the chance to be children from my work and sacrifices and will never know they are starting much further upstream than I ever had the chance to, and hopefully travel much further downstream much easier than I. This is the balance between our lifetimes. I pray that this is the hope of every father. And now, the current work can be overwhelming, and progress seems slow or nonexistent, but I must look at where I started and the condition of the stream when I began this journey and the effort to leave these children something to gauge their beginning. That is the true measure in the stream and in one's life. Measure from where you started to truly see how far you have come.

As if this beautiful place could not become any more spectacular, it does when the children are here. When I am graced with their presence, the clocks stop ticking, the minutes have no wings, all the church bells ring continuously through the mountains in joyous harmony; the sun never sets and always warms my face, there is no pain, no rain, no birches dare lose a leaf except to become a traveling leaf-boat; the breeze is always soft and warm against my neck, the day always rises to greet me with thunderous applause, and the stream smiles and welcomes them with tears. I never fail to embrace every moment whether it be them catching fish or placing band aids on hornet stings; they are all priceless and travel us downstream with brilliant, shared stories. There is a time for serious understanding and then there is a time to allow our eyes to widen and wonder, and the stream understands these connections. She has entertained countless lives and felt countless footsteps of countless innocent children over countless decades. She has kindly welcomed them all, held a place and time for them all, and has asked only we think of her not simply as an object for use. Now she is part of our family.

9-2-21

Laurel Creek and the mountain North side view
Pen, ink, pencil on paper
Mark T. Wright

Hurricane Ida continued past the gulf moving north northeast through the Carolinas dumping three inches of rain in the mountains over two days. The stream swelled but did not flood as it had the previous week when we had two inches of rainfall in twelve hours. By observing the stream in extreme conditions, I learn how she is tested by the excess amount of water. About one half of the structures held fast as I built them, and helped the stream control the effects of rising water. These structures, constantly modified by the water and molded as part of the stream in a combined effort, seek balance. I worked on the waterfall by the bridge again, and now it is a stair step cascade so fish can communicate up and downstream easily. I have worked about three hundred feet of stream to help achieve this goal of better communication and flow. I see this as a partnership and collaborative effort between the water, stream, and myself. But I never really know every condition, every drop, every turn, every move of nature. But as the Zen saying goes, "Thinking we know shows we know nothing, knowing we don't know shows we know."

The basic bank structure is sufficient at bending the water at this point, and I need to shift my focus on the depth of each pool and on developing the main channel. Eventually, after the water and I modify the stream shape, I will feather out the stones and lesson the severity of the bank slopes. But for now, it is necessary to keep a rigid structure to redirect the current to the center of the stream bed. The water and stream are cooperating tentatively up to this point and seem to be entertaining my suggestions and solutions. Sometimes I work with the water to help mold the stream form and other times I work with the stream to form the water, and always they work independently from me to improve or undo our efforts. But we always work together to achieve the goal of balance. I need to make a huge deep pool in one spot where the flow and structure are right. I have worked on various sections that are adequate with deeper runs and with boulders I placed in strategic locations as structure on the bottom. Surprise is inevitable, welcomed and is the joy of the practice.

Last evening, I watched a video on trout habitats and activity filmed under water, in a stream, and at multiple locations and seasons. (Not as engaging as *The Godfather*, but interesting nonetheless since I am in the thick of things in the water.) This was scientific research of stream dynamics as field observations in real time and varying conditions. Although the film focused on trout habitat, the surprising conclusion for me was that trout are not just where we have always suspected as traditionally educated informed anglers and stream life is as complex and complicated as any city with its multiple overlapping and transparent layers of diversity. Simply put, this is because of the varying currents at all depths and locations, structure, and water temperature within any stretch of stream water. These variations in current are unpredictable since the slightest variation in stream structure changes the conditions and can make it palatable for a multitude of entities, including the trout, to hold and wait for food and become food.

Currents vary from top to bottom in as little as six inches of water. As flyfishing anglers, when we cast our subsurface flies in the stream, we really have no idea where our fly is located under the surface since the current is so varied. It moves with the current and the lure could be at any level in any direction independent from the surface indicator. Additionally, the research showed that food floating by a trout can occur at any level under the water, at any spot at any time and the fish are there but may not be interested. Fluvial theory helps us understand stream dynamics in general and at an ideal academic level, but the myriad of factors varying in each cubic inch of stream produce unpredictable chaotic patterns.

Variations in the currents are obvious when studying stream dynamics, in real time, in the stream. The water has been clear as glass and I can observe the surface current in locations swiftly flowing, bubbling full of oxygen, and just four inches below I feel the current slow to almost half that speed. I can watch objects floating in the current at various levels moving along at completely different paces. Then I observed a boulder located in the path of the stream. The dynamics change radically. The current sweeps by the boulder at full speed and we expect the current and motion on the upstream side to equal the downstream side, the Bernoulli principle. But behind the boulder on the downstream side there is beautiful foaming bubbling white water on the surface and sediment gathered on the stream bottom, and there is a slower backflow of water in the opposite direction of the stream. The water does not "stick" to the downstream side of the boulder, as high pressure creates a reduced water velocity opening the current on the downstream side of the boulder. We anglers call this "pocket water" and it is where to locate holding trout waiting in slower water, conserving energy watching the faster water pass by with food for the taking. The trout knows this magic. On the upstream side complicated curls of foaming water halted by the boulder, churn, and splash against the boulder, creating a split and slow, push back into the stream. We were taught about the

Bernoulli's principle and the physics of the airplane wing, but flow in a stream does not happen in a vacuum under controlled conditions and the boulders and stones vary, drag is present, water level varies, viscosity varies, incredibly magical asymmetry occurs with turbulence and creates mystical beautiful chaos as with every leaf or snowflake.

This incredible chaotic action simply does not happen in two dimensions as seen from the surface. We initially see behind the boulder on the downstream side, a swirl of current curling back in circular patterns at the surface then reconnects with the main current. But again, this phenomenon happens in three dimensions plus time, and adds enormous complexity to the stream dynamics combining fast main surface water, slower bottom water, swirling water rotating in the opposite direction at the surface, and still at the bottom. Then add the varying width of the stream, underwater rocks and boulders, and steeper and shallower falls and there is a beautiful complex dance occurring at every location in the stream that rivals the intensity of New York City at rush hour.

But it is extremely simple in certain ways. The only absolute in the complex dance is gravity. The water is seeking the lowest point along its journey, intuitively drawn, to meet the other family members to reach their ultimate end and sea level. The magic of the stream transforms the simple absolute action of gravity into an elegant romp by means of water volume and the degree of grade change and the stream geometry over time. I can build the same form in multiple locations but never achieve the exact results. One adjustment of any element radically affects a different outcome, spatially and temporally. The stream is truly a living entity.

I am working to complete my son's room so I have not had time to work on the stream as much as I would like. But every morning and evening I stop to observe and listen to the stream if only for a brief time. The rain has also made it impossible to work since the stream swells and flows sometimes at a dangerous pace. But now after the rain has stopped the water reduces quickly, and it allows me to evaluate and plan. I visualize the changes I could make and act out the results in my mind as a rehearsed play. Improvisation is the only certainty. I watch the main channel flow and its subtle switches to understand the surface and subsurface currents and evaluate what is the least I can do to accomplish a beautiful balance; and what I can leave to the water and stream to complete. This requires a leap of faith and a letting go of immediacy and instant gratification. It is like adding landscaping. We must plan for the long game and not the immediate visual, or we might plant an oak tree three feet from the main house. Immediately the oak looks perfect but in a few years the tree has outgrown its area and will not yield to the house. So, I try to create an environment encouraging the water to lessen erosion and clearing silt at locations conducive to good stream health. This is part of the constant conversation along with millions of observations processed before moving the next stone. The patient search continues.

9-3-21

I mostly finished Harry's room. I decided to work on the west side of the stream today. I was taking a break while in the water, and a green hummingbird came up to me about three feet away. I made eye contact as I heard the buzz of his wings and felt the vibrations from his hovering. It is the same one that visits me on occasion while I am working in the stream. It is as if he was saying, "Well, soon most of the flowers will be gone. What are you going to do about it?" It was a sign to post hummingbird feeders for the little guys for the fall to aid them in fueling up for their journey across the gulf.

These tiny fliers are a joyful site and bring a smile to my face whenever they visit. They show off with chest out flexing their huge pectoral muscles flying forward, backwards sideways, any way they need to gather nectar from the flowers and feeder. When they come close, I can almost hear their tiny heartbeat, two hundred times faster than mine. Their eyesight is strong, and they seek out colorful flowers, especially in the red color range to dive into and lick the nectar from deep in the plant. Maybe coincidence, maybe design by nature, but most other insects including the bees in the neighborhood cannot see red and are less drawn to the same flowers as the hummingbird. I see the bees and hummingbirds jostle for position on the white trumpet vine flowers but few if any bees on the feeder with red sugar water.

I focused on an area in the stream that I had exposed around a huge ten-foot diameter boulder that sets six feet above the water surface. The stream, cleared completely around the ten-foot diameter boulder, allows the water to flow on the right side helping to wash the silt away. I dug a twelve-foot half-moon shape route around the right side of the boulder about twelve inches deep from the mainstream to the deep hole on the opposite side augmenting the natural flow that exists. I am not convinced that this is the right solution here, so I proceed with trepidation. This is a confusing area, even for the stream, and water flowing around the right side of the boulder becomes non-existent in dry summer and becomes active only as an overflow as the water rises. This huge boulder acts as a large island stop for debris and some plants and I believe will continue to do so and eventually fill in the area to the right of the structure. We will see. I also worked the flats into a steady flow instead of a waterfall. This will allow communication again and enrich the water. As I was doing this, I removed rocks from the bottom main run to deepen and clear it and placed them in areas against the bank that were eroding and undercut. This will displace water to the center stream flow and eliminate dead spots and eroded banks.

As I relocate the stones, the results are almost immediate and I can feel the water shift, rise around my legs, and flow from the dead areas to the main channel run. This will help increase the current and help transport the sediment away. The water level rises quickly, maintains for the duration of the work, but then retreats slightly teasing me with the illusion of permanence. So now in this short spot there is a cascading waterfall, flats and a good water flow that communicates to the other parts of the stream. I am hopeful that nature will help me deepen these areas by the flow of water over time, but I will go back and do more work. The deep hole, now fed with oxygen rich water, invigorated by the cascading action of the current and falls provides a healthy environment for the fish to thrive in this area.

This entire process has transformed me into an overzealous advocate for the water, and I am less tolerant than I expected of people who do not believe the same. This section of the stream cuts through my property and I own the property on both sides of the stream. And as the beautiful spiritual belief of the Cherokee native Americans goes, no one can own the water; they simply inherit it. No one can own the water, as no one can own the air and the breeze. And as the sap in the trees, the blood in our veins, and the water in the stream, are all connected as a life-giving force that we share. But people must traverse my property to reach the stream and they are on my property if they step foot in the stream in this area. They are standing on my property as their feet touch the bottom of the stream.

Two weeks ago, when the children were here for a few days, we were leaving to go into town to eat dinner, and my children pointed out a myriad of piano wing butterflies gathered near the driveway on the ground concentrated in one small spot like vultures on carrion. As we looked closer, we found the gutted carcass of a rainbow trout at the bottom of my drive at the bridge. Someone came onto the property, took a fish, and decapitated it, gutted it there then left. This happened exceedingly early on a Saturday morning, so the perpetrator did their worst before we discovered the damage. I had a suspect.

This disappointed me, that the fish survived the heat of summer in the worked stream, and someone had the audacity to butcher it on the spot on the property. I tell Harry, "It's important to take fish out only if you need to eat them and not just because you can. Some fish have a soul contract for this purpose, but others do not. So we fish, we catch, we admire their beauty, we experience their energy, we thank them for the time and this momentary gift…and then we release them." And killing and gutting this beautiful creature as they did, was a brutal and selfish act exposing a person empty of reverence and respect for the stream life and the land.

Laurel Creek flowing gently while being rehabilitated.
Pencil and pen on paper
Mark T. Wright

Earlier in the week, I witnessed a man, long grey hair protruding out the sides of his blue tattered ball cap, rough couple of days beard growth, belly pushing out the front of his worn and dirty overalls, high green rubber boots, his dented grey Ford Pinto parked just behind him at the gravel road, fishing under the bridge with a spinning rod and using shrimp bait that looks like small food pellets. These resemble the pellets that the state wildlife agency feeds the fish before they release them to the streams. The state stocked the stream with rainbow and brown trout just two days ago. I watched him as he cast into the current under the bridge, into clear water on a bright sunny day after a light rain. He proceeded to catch the small trout, pulled the fish out of the water suspended from the hook in its mouth, managed it brutally, both arms bent resting on his belly as he pulled the fish close to him to remove the hook, held the trout tightly in his left hand and struck its head efficiently with the rod butt to kill it and then placed in his creel. He caught three fish in an hour while I was there watching him before I said a word. He was on the south side of the stream while I stood on the north side.

"How you doing?" I said loudly above the stream roar.

"Great, just castin' and catchin'…three so far."

"You live around here?"

"Just up near Beaver Creek.…you live here now?" he said with apprehension in his voice.

"Yes sir, just bought the place from Wayne, a few months ago and I am the new owner."

"Yeah? I did a lotta work for ole' Wayne on the house."

"Really?"

"Yep, did most of the stucco work then a lot of other stuff over the years, still looks pretty good," he said with an unearned swagger as if speaking to someone uneducated in construction who could not verify his exaggerated claim and as if that earned him a place at the property's round table.

"Is that right," I said. The stucco work was an atrocity and some of the worst work I had seen in forty years in the construction business; and the work was bad when it was done.

"Yeah, I was up at the other bridge a few days ago and caught twelve (fish) upstream. Yeah, if I had caught twenty and cooked 'em, my old lady would eat 'em all. She just loves trout."

I had less than flattering, not fair I admit, images of him and his "old lady" at the supper table devouring twenty trout. He laughed and said it in a chummy braggadocious sort of way, as if expecting that I would be impressed and buy into the good old boy attempt and comradery; I did not. The state stocks fish at that bridge and I suspect he was waiting like a bald, big-eyed, hook beaked turkey vulture to pull them out as fast as the state put the fish in the water.

"I thought the state limit is seven fish per day?" I said rhetorically knowing I was speaking to a person who was a prime example and who reeked of Dante's deadly sin of gluttony and who knew very well the laws on keeping seven trout per day per person in North Carolina. There was no reply, but his eyes widened, and his face dropped suddenly and had a startled look of having one's hand caught in the trout jar.

"I think it is time for you to move on. You are on my property, and I think you have caught enough fish here. The idea is for everyone to enjoy these waters. So please just move on. There are other places you can go." He knew and packed up and left without a word.

That next morning, I spoke to fish biologist Mr. Johnson at the department of fish and wildlife of NC District 7. He was calm, informed and spoke with a charmingly friendly North Carolina accent that attested he had at least lived here for most of his life, if not had been born here. He oversees the public waters in nine counties in his district. This is no small task.

"Mr. Johnson," I said, "I don't know if you can help me, but I just purchased a piece of property in Watauga County. The stream goes through my property for about eight hundred fifty feet, and I own both sides of the stream. You stock above and below me there on a delayed harvest schedule. But I have an issue with people coming onto my property and not just taking fish but not respecting the property or the privilege of fishing there."

"I have heard this a lot over the last few years," he said.

"I don't mean to be a prick, but someone told me they took twelve fish at one spot and the same guy gutted a fish on my driveway."

"You're not, we get calls like this every day about people doing the same thing on a person's property where we stock," he said.

"Well, how do you deal with it?"

"We don't have an answer. These people wait for us to stock and take every fish out they can. We can't do anything about it since that is the law during that period and it is impossible to police every location," he said.

"I would consider leaving it open to public fishing if you will still stock it and make it catch and release only with a flyrod. That way everyone gets to fish and at least people will respect the water and put the fish back. You already do this at the Watauga River and many other places in the state."

He went on, "It would be difficult to change that. It would have to be the general assembly that would vote on it, and it would be hard to just section that part of the stream off."

"OK, Mr. Johnson, I guess I will close the stream to the public and put-up signs."

"Mr. Wright, that is perfectly OK, and we have owners do it all the time. I'll inform the field guys and just go ahead and put your signs over top of ours and I'll inform the stocking crew to stop."

"Mr. Johnson, I am sorry, but I was pushed a little too far."

"Mr. Wright, we understand, and I wish the circumstances were different, but we get it."

"Thank you, sir," I said and wished him luck and thanked him for his patience and understanding.

I ordered the no fishing and no trespassing signs, and I put them in various places along the stream for the length of the property. A neighbor up the hill saw me, stopped, and said, "You do that, and it will make people mad, and we don't like new people moving in and closing off fishing and changing things." It appears that they told Tom and Liz, residents of forty years, that they were new people also here since they were not kinfolk of the original settlers in this neighborhood, or of a clan from Watauga County. I said, "Didn't you tell me you were building a pond on your property up the hill there, fed by a mountain stream? I'll be happy to let everyone know that you said it is ok for them to fish on your property in your pond. I am sure you do not mind since you do not want to close off fishing." She left in a huff, and I am assuming she is not inviting me to the spring fondue party up the hill.

Later in the week I decided to test the waters and make a few casts into the stream since I had not wet a line in months. I put on a flashback pheasant tail I tied over the winter, my go to nymph, on a #6 tippet, and my two weight seven-foot six-inch rod with a turtle knot and a small foam indicator and made fifty roll casts into a heavy riffle that feeds into a deeper run. I began the cast short to the stream then lengthened the cast each time and at the same time fanning the casts trying to get the nymph down in every spot I could. Soft water, fast water in the middle of the fast riffles, all places since I knew that fish could be anywhere and that my nymph is not that predictable once it hits the under-surface currents. I was optimistic that there were holdovers and survivors from the earlier spring. After fifty unproductive casts I just relegated the effort to practicing my presentation and roll casting in tight areas. On the fifty first cast into the strongest part of the current and foaming water, I felt that adrenaline charged tug on the end of my line, saw it, and felt it straighten, the rod tip bent as I lifted my right arm straight up to mimic the statue of liberty opposing the leader that was moving away from me, watched the fish jerk and shutter and throw the hook as the line went slack like the air from a birthday balloon, and I lost the fish.

So, I waited about twenty minutes to let the water rest from my disturbance and started the routine again but set the nymph about four inches deeper. The stream is not that deep, and this section is only three feet maximum at a small run. I can visualize this magical dance beneath water where the trout sees the nymph in the faster moving water and has a noticeably brief time to decide whether to strike or let a potential food source float by. Was the presentation sufficient to fool the fish into striking, thus beginning the dance? There are anglers who say they have caught fish on bare gold hook with the right presentation. Is there a fish there at all, and was the earlier action an illusion? Since the current here is stronger, foaming riffles and water depth distorts any view beneath the water surface, so site fishing is not possible.

Another fifty casts in every inch of water and I finally felt that magnificent tug again, and performing the same practiced routine burned in my muscle memory over thirty years, I lifted the rod straight up. I lift straight up because a trout will normally strike the fly and turn down to return to its holding place readying itself to strike again at floating food. So, if I lift straight up the hook is set easily with the help of the fish. This time the fish gods smiled upon me, and I hooked a nice twelve-inch rainbow trout in a perfectly orchestrated composition between me and the fish. It was feistier than I expected. But since I worked on the stream resulting in a faster and cleaner water flow and more oxygenation, it is maintaining cooler water just around sixty-eight degrees during even the hottest months, and more than likely, is resulting in healthier spunkier fish.

After a quick fight as not to stress the fish too much, I brought the beautiful creature closer to me at the bank. I kept it in the water not wanting to contaminate its body with human touch, if possible, while admiring the brilliant rainbow colors, asked it to calm down and cease the splashing and rolling so we could part quickly, said, "Thank you for this moment," and released the fish without touching it. I bent the barb off the hook, making for an easy release. This was a huge surprise and a guarded precious gift. I went back to working the upper part of the stream again about one hundred feet upstream and then later came back and repeated the exercise and caught another eight-inch rainbow, smaller than before, but still a pleasant surprise. Overall, I made one hundred fifty casts in the same area yielding two fish. This was a good day.

I pray to the fish gods that this is a sign that the work I am doing is yielding a healthy stream. By concentrating the water, reducing the erosion, deepening the channels, creating under water structures, varying the flow of water, making communicating routes, adding riffles and runs, helping reduce the water temperature (even in August), creating deep holes for holding, getting rid of the sediment, eliminating the full damns, creating diverters; it seems like the water is becoming fuller with life. If these fish are alive and thriving in the warmest months, it means the water temperature is cool enough for them to survive and there is a food source here for them and a food source for that food source. It is simple really. There is still a huge amount of work to do, but the stream and water are speaking to me and letting me know where they need adjustments and where they have no intention of going. And life returning to the water is letting us know we are on the right track. It is a conversation of repair, and water and stream know I am trying to help by following their lead, but the water and the stream have minds of their own. Beautiful entities speaking if we only listen.

Harry and Margaret Annie exploring in the stream.
No work today!

Chapter VII

9-7-21

The children came up this Labor Day weekend and we pack a month worth of living into four days here in the mountains. We hike the stream, the mountains, and I try to let them unwind and enjoy the peace here. We got Harry an Xbox with a game he wanted called *Plants vs Zombies*. He is such a good boy and does great in school, so it is easy to try to make him happy especially since he is at a new school with new peer pressure. The COVID-19 disaster is looming over the lives of these children as the restrictions have forced home learning and remote teaching devoid of human interaction with teachers or peers. It makes us all shiver and recall the polio epidemic of the late nineteen forties and fifties in the United States and how children were dying from the disease until Salk developed a vaccine around 1955. Margaret Annie is painting and trying to get into a magnet art school in Louisville. She is such a good big sister and Harry just adores her. It is humorous, as I was trying to make conversation and asked, "Have you seen my artwork on my new website?"

"Of course, I follow you on Instagram," she said.

I do not even follow myself on Instagram and her saying this floored me to tears. This trip was a bit subdued, and they were content to rest after the likes.

The children left yesterday, and I went into workaholic self-protection mode, cleaned, and did laundry and then worked in the stream until five pm. It was a long day, but I needed to stay busy pushing myself to the point of exhaustion, fighting to fill the huge emotional void crushing my heart after the children leave. It is a predicable routine of overwhelming joy being with them as they fill this house with the beautiful energy from their magnificent souls; and a horrible crash of sadness as the house empties when they return to Louisville. Although I know I will see them again soon, and as sure as the sun comes up every day, I cannot help the predictable deflating loneliness I feel when I drop them off. They resume their life as if nothing happened and shift between worlds effortlessly because they know, primally, that they are loved. After they return to their home in Kentucky, the stream work is a cathartic exercise that saves me from my own pathetic pouting and emptiness echoing through the house. I miss the innocent joy they carry, and I miss the humbleness I feel in their presence.

Back to the stream, I continued to fill in the undercut banks using material excavated from the main channel of the stream. By simple displacement and taking material from the main channel, I deepen the stream while at the same time building the bank edges. This involves taking the rocks and sand from the center engorged areas and filling in the eroded parts of the bank so that they slope gently toward the center of the stream. As I progress with the work there are visual hints suggested by the stream as to what she wants to become. So, to really see, not just to look, and effect a positive change, it takes continuous practice, and flexibility with the design before any action takes place. Sometimes the solution is painfully obvious. Other times it takes long meditation and lengthy observation, like the heron stalking prey in the stream, for the answer to reveal itself. But always the patient search is the practice.

The stream now looks like a potpourri of riffles runs and shallow pools. I have achieved a consistent depth from six inches to about eighteen inches and I will try to achieve a depth of three feet at the falls behind the cottage. Hopefully, the stream will help me enhance these areas now that I have planted the seed, developed a consistent center channel, and deepened the pools. As I work my way upstream, I have a plan after studying the streams' movements in low and high water. When I work up stream it will impact the lower section, and as I have said, this is the perfect example of the butterfly effect. To date, the impact has been positive and has helped simplify aspects of both upper and lower sections. By creating a subtle meandering shape with a consistent center channel, in addition to the varied bottom configuration, it adds diversity to the stream and during a flood event it helps dissipate the energy of the raging water by reducing the velocity. I am trying to create a dynamic stream, keeping the proportions consistent along its run. This shape increases the distance that the water will travel and at the same time reduces the slope of the channel like an accessible ramp to a building. This seems obvious, but at the beginning the stream crested in the center, was a shallow to almost dry form, and was a straight run. We will see.

I must follow the stream's lead and build all the meandering structural movement into the existing confined terrain. This is the most difficult, but I believe the most effective way to facilitate permanent balance. I have outlined the structural edges and defined the parameters of the general stream course. The great Italian architectural genius Leo Ricci, who I had the privilege of knowing as a teacher, is always in the back of my mind when designing anything. "Structure!" he would say. "Show me the structure." I can then edit out certain sections of the work after the water has decided if it is happy with the structure. The other option would be to mimic the process recently executed at Cove Creek and reroute the stream with heavy equipment. This is not acceptable to me. I have followed her advice, have done what she has advised, and I believe I have redirected her to where she desires to go. I must be continually vigilant since the plan is to help the stream become healthy, vibrant, and balanced in the lowest water level, and to assist her with preparation to manage the highest water level with minimum stress and damage. In that light, I have ideas to achieve this balance, but again nature lets me know.

9-13-21

I spent all Saturday missing the children terribly and working myself in a frenzy of exhaustion. I have my moments of loneliness here in the mountains, mostly after the children come then leave. Work and education have always been my crutch and my haven when faced with any emotional issues. But when I am with them, I realize the work moves aside and makes a space for them willingly and is content to wait for me as an old friend. Their absence is a grand motivator to seek solace in the work. But that always makes for a good night's sleep and a ridiculously painful body. Today I am too exhausted to write, and simply making dinner is a major task. However, I'll be the first to admit that I need to put a governor on the time working in the stream, or any physical labor, of about four or five hours to protect myself from myself.

9-16-21

After struggling through discussions with my attorney concerning a frivolous lawsuit brought against the company, I went out to work the stream yesterday to wash the slime from my hands. I have been pushing myself to complete work and my body is hurting worse than usual. I walked to the bridge and looked out upstream at the work I completed, and I did not realize the number of rocks and boulders I moved. Although half of the upstream section was well under way, the effort seemed almost insignificant compared to the total scope of completing the entire length of the stream.

I need to begin work renovating the cottage. The arborist removed the trees that were choking out the light around the building. It is amazing the breadth it took and how well it is breathing now. There is a severe labor shortage across the country and in the area, and I cannot find people to work. COVID-19 cases are increasing. I worry about the children. I finally found a photographer who is coming to shoot and document my artwork next week. I have needed to do this for years.

I worked on the west side of the stream again and am pinching the edges inward and deepening the center to focus on the flow of water. The stream has widened and flattened out and the bank has flattened on one side. So, there is no channel, no actual run, no variation, no communication, only a flat wide area that evaporates water and cannot sustain fish. I think I do not have enough existing material to fill the banks so I may need to call for delivery of #1's or #3's to build the volume to stop further erosion and then place the stream stone on top. It is difficult to reach these areas with a truck, and the remoteness may force me to move the stone by hand and a wheelbarrow.

I have removed heavier, larger boulders from a center line I observed as the natural flow of the stream to allow a channel to start. I studied the stream quietly and solemnly and discovered the natural flow of the water and how she wants to move. I can see the ancillary flows off the main desired flow. Since this stream has a consistent but exceedingly small amount of water volume, especially in the summer months, I am concentrating the water flow and creating a narrower deeper stream. Granted, in a heavy flood, as from the results of a hurricane, all bets are off, compromising the structure of the stream. With five inches of rain in thirty-six hours earlier this year the stream flooded out of control. But when the next event produced four inches of rain over three days the stream flooded but the structure stayed in place and was resilient as the water receded.

As Eisenhower said, "In preparing for battle I have always found that plans are useless, but planning is indispensable." Working this stream is a team effort with her, water, and the other partners of nature. She collaborates with me, or plots against me in a humorous way like Zeus with mere mortals. She suggests where she would like to go and where she can go. Then at a whim of nature, changes and shifts at my expense. Unless I wanted to bulldoze the entire stream and start over, which would be insane, brutal and nonsense, it is a specialized conversation. There are natural hints that are there for me to discover. Boulders covered for years show their faces after each rush of water across them, if you look, rub, and dig. Others, already exposed, I move to help displace water and squeeze the bank edge down.

Since I have begun work, I have observed the water temperature maintaining in these summer months at sixty-five degrees. Not perfect, but I believe it will either drop in temperature or remain consistent at this temperature as I continue work. This will sustain rainbows and browns but is at the upper temperature limit to support brookies. In my heart, I believe at the beginning of time, this was a brook trout stream, small, consistent, cool, bolder bottoms with gravel and sand, and a great overhead canopy of trees and cover. I think over the years this wonder has evolved into a sad limping shallow form.

I am achieving about a foot of water, worse case in the areas I am working, and am getting up to two to three feet and more depth in areas. Ideally, mother nature will help and eventually carve out these areas with increased water velocity with every rain. I have achieved this depth when the water level is low. The goal is to achieve at least these depths at the worse time and slowest water flow. I have been conscious of creating paths of water so the fish can move upstream and have placed huge boulders strategically to shield the current and create underwater cover.

The east side of the stream section requires the most work. The water level becomes shallow there and I need to deepen these areas. I have been concentrating on the stream because soon the water will be too cold for me to work. Once the water temperature reaches the low fifties my hands will not be able to function efficiently in the chilly water. When this occurs, I will start work rebuilding the bridge rails and the steps up from the lower bridge area to the house eighty feet up the mountain and concentrate on the house renovation.

My hand crafted wood joinery at the bridge.

Casting a small fly into the stream now as a test, draws the small fry minnows. I cannot tell what type of fish they are, but wishing they were small brook trout or rainbows that were born in the stream. Honestly, it does not matter. They are inhabiting the structures I built and the holes I created. Casting into the proper areas with an extremely soft touch and a good short drift gets a hit on a dry fly. So, there is life in these areas now and that is a good sign. If the fish like it so far, the stream gods are smiling on me.

Coaxing, prodding, working, and begging the stream into balance is playing a patient long game and swaying hand in hand in a slow dance with her. The process has short term gains and long-term effects. The stream structure, partially configured, will take years of forming and reforming to erase the years of neglect and damage before returning to balance. The extreme weather will continue; it appears to be the new normal. We will try to work together to reclaim a healthy alliance between me, she, the water, and the life that she supports, while preparing for extremes. I am learning from doing.

9-21-21

I worked in the stream three times since the last entry. Each time I drove myself to a point of glorious physical exhaustion working until dark, and at the end of the day I could hardly eat. It was painful just to close my hands, cook dinner and shower. Working on the west side of the stream is a Herculean task and as I barely scratch the surface of what needs to be accomplished, I see, at the same time, huge gains. It is like a mountain that appears clearer to the climber from a distance as opposed to when on the cliff. Stepping back and seeing the overall amount of work completed is humbling. Fifty percent of the work is place holding using boulders to mold and reroute the water temporarily, until I establish a synthesis of form, flow, depth, curvature, and mass that seems right for each section to approach balance. I am moving sand and gravel and small rocks, a shovel at a time, and one boulder at a time, slowly and methodically. It is amazing that minor changes I make in the stream often lead to major outcomes—if I'm patient. Every step in the stream alters events even if they are imperceivable to us, but the salamanders know. It is a dance I do with the stream, and she follows to a limited degree. The rain finally came, and the work is holding up well and the stream is helping reroute the water in step. But it also emphasizes the amount of work there is to do. Years of neglect and flooding eroded the side banks and flattened the stream so there was no balanced habitat and little water flow.

I am first laying out the correct curvature of the new stream side to help vary the flow. Then I took boulders about eighteen to twenty-four inches in diameter and using these I built up a twenty-four-inch-high border above the water to shape the new bank edge. I then fill this area between the stones and the bank soil with the stream gravel, sand and soil establishing a new riparian area. I have run out of material and cannot use the stream stone to get enough fill to reach the bank. So, I may need rip rap and then either stone on top, or soil and plant the edges again. At any rate, the undertaking is monumental but necessary.

The rain helps to increase the water volume and velocity and carve out the center of the stream like a concave rounded wood chisel rolling shavings off to create a fluid groove exposing the rocky and gravel bottom. At the upper waterfall I will need to deepen the stream to make sure the water stays inside the run. It is overflowing the flattened bank now. When I get to this area again, I can deepen it easily and lay stream stones on the bank to constrict and accelerate water flow. Every rainfall teaches me where I have failed, succeeded, and where the idea is good but needs adjusting. So far, I am running about 70/30 on the work success ratio. The thirty percent of the work requires working and adjusting the stream from the results of successful work in the upper and lower sections and tailoring the changes to the whim of the water.

I have no statistical reference to determine with any accurate margin of error what a 'good' success rate should be for the stream work. I have no reference for establishing a lifespan for the modifications, or what needs to be maintenance. I have no predictions for the longevity of the structures, or how they will morph into other creatures absorbed by the stream. Water flowing is water flowing, and cooler water in the summer months flowing, is cooler water flowing in the summer months. The success rate seems irrelevant, and the only measure of success is the smiling salamanders, crawdads, and freshwater snails who I believe will let the fish know.

Between Monk and Mozart
Pen, ink, pencil and gesso on paper
Mark T. Wright

This is good, I believe, since the water amount is finite, and I am adjusting the stream to maintain consistent water flow during hot and dry months. With the deeper runs established and the banks stabilized, the stream should adjust and run again at all levels...of course, except when massive flooding occurs. This may begin to happen more often as the climate changes and becomes more erratic. However, the stream managed the water from the last flood with less damage. It seems that by trying to work the stream and thinking of it as a fish habitat helps the overall balance, staying erosion even at the most extreme case. The way to succeed is by being in the stream; listening to the water; seeing the route that it wants to take, then making an educated plan of the changes that will positively affect it without losing all its natural beauty.

It is a musical composition of chaos theory. To paraphrase Stravinsky, "All the elements exist, but the elements must be properly assembled to elevate the composition to art," the art of the stream. I believe that art and nature are operating from the same laws. It takes the patient search to find the combinations of stone placement, displacement, shape, and depth searching for the balance in the stream. The miracle is the fluidity of the water and its exciting unpredictability that adds an additional element to the composition as we attempt to have everything working in concert.

But the music that is emerging in these waters is more complex than any manmade opus. And unlike Stravinsky, I am working with nature as a partner in the composition and make only humble assumptions on how I can tune the stream and orchestrate the concerto. So far, the stream is working in concert with the water and with less discourse. I see life reinvigorated and joining the band. From the small salamander to the darting sculpins, the flat nymph to the scurrying crawdad to the hoovering damselflies, the stoic birch trees (which cannot be stifled forever as they drop their leaves), contribute to the living composition the stream life seems to be singing.

I'm maneuvering in the stream with dueling shovels.

Chapter IX

9-22-21

There are three twelve-inch diameter corrugated pipe culverts located beneath the road within the eight-hundred-foot run of stream inside the property boundaries, with countless more up and downstream directing water from the surrounding areas and gravel road into the stream like small capillaries feeding the main vein. One outlet is located downstream near the bridge. This pipe stops fifty yards from the stream edge and has caused erosion of the fifty-yard area into a muddy ditch that deposits vast amounts of sediment into the stream at its confluence. This discharge pipe is manageable, and I will try to encourage a water garden system, modified, to help filter the runoff prior to it hitting the stream. I have placed twenty tons of stone there on top of eight tons of gravel to help reduce the erosion and silt deposits. Essentially, I have created a mini-detention pond, capturing the runoff, slowing it down, reducing the erosion, reducing the deposit of sediment, and dispersing the runoff exit into the stream. A bio garden is the best idea since plants will eventually cover the stone and hide it under a blanket of flora with roots helping hold the area in place during heavy runoff. I have excavated a drop from the culvert opening to the stream and my version of Eco Pond appears to at least filter the runoff before reaching the stream. The last rain forcing water through the pipe slowed from the rip rap, hit the enlarged pond area, filtered the water, and then dispersed it over a widened area of additional stone reducing the mud and silt before hitting the stream.

The other two inlets are problematic. One is located upstream at the far end of the property line and the other downstream at the lower end of the property at an elevation three feet higher above the stream level. They protrude twenty-four inches out from the edge of the road and spill water indiscriminately into the stream as an uncontrolled waterfall. These are the number one culprits of the limestone fines making their way into the stream directly, clouding the water and turning it into the grey mass immediately after a summer rain. When this happens, I witness this rolling ghostly grey finely particle mass moving downstream mimicking the movement of a marching haboob or like dust following on the heels of stampeding horses changing the watercolor to grey. It is not possible to construct filters at these locations, and the only possibility would be to cut the pipes shorter and deposit larger boulders below it to disperse the water. This would be a monumental task. This upstream outlet is extremely important since it begins the stream work and is at the extreme upstream edge of the property. Its cantilevered form protrudes from the bank a bit, so there is no erosion, and the waterfall hits the boulders three feet below before hitting the stream. The downside for both outlets is there is no filter from whatever water runoff from the adjacent properties and no screening of sediment before it hits the stream. The stream water is healthy, so I am assuming the glory of the mountains is helping to filter the water before it reaches the stream.

I am optimistic that trout will return in the stream as a test measuring the difference the work has made. The smaller creatures are thriving and have come back to the water paving the way for the trout. We know major factors correlating with the trout habitat seem to be the amount of forest area and pasture adjacent to and surrounding the stream. We know lower water temperature and water purity are basic factors encouraging trout habitat. We know the basic things, but further studies were interesting determining factors such as adjacent road frontage and makeup that were not significant and showed no correlation in the trout population survival. So, academic studies confirm our general simple knowledge that, primarily, the little critters' habitat must be of lower water temperature and more highly oxygenated clean water.

The other factors that cannot be readily measured but provide an ideal habitat are existential such as cover placement, riffle length and frequency, underwater terrain, adjustment in water direction and depth. We must be pragmatic and think like the trout while listening to the stream telling us all the possibilities and the myriad of structural combinations to achieve balance. And it will tell you! The solace in all this evaluation and effort is that if we strive to make these streams sustainable environments for the trout, we will also achieve a beautiful environment for us and help the stream be as it desires to be. The compromise is only the amount of work I can do physically and economically in the years I have remaining on this planet. It pains me to say that because there should be no compromising, but I am only one man with limited years to help this creature seek balance. My time is but a speck of dust in a boxcar measure of time in the eyes of the stream, six life cycles in the eyes of the brook trout, and hopefully, one good lifetime spent as a baseline for my children to continue stewardship.

10-1-21

I was working diligently in the upper section of stream to beat the rain, head down, confined in the deeper walled bank area so the road and its dust from cars running on the gravel are ten feet above me. I stopped and took a breath, looked up and at the road, and above me standing motionless like a turkey vulture perched on a dead tree limb, was a thin pale faced, white long-haired apparition in a knee length pink down coat... my neighbor from half a mile upstream. She clearly saw I was working but stopped and spoke.

"Hello, I...just...road." I could only make out every other word due to the sound of cascading water echoing off the higher bank wall, so I stopped, dropped the shovel and, out of courtesy, approached the bank below her. Looking up at the ghost in a pink coat I said, "I'm sorry I could not hear a word you said, I'm Mark."

"Hi, I'm your neighbor, Beverly Winston, "Bev," I live in the white house on the right up the road."

"Nice to meet you," I said, but I had no idea which house she was speaking about.

"I was taking my walk, to help my hip problem and was wondering what you were doing. I knew Wayne sold the house, so you are the new owner. Welcome to the neighborhood. I take my walk here every day except Sunday. I have seen you working so I thought I would finally stop to say hello. What are you doing there? I lost my barn in the flood of 2004-05. That flood was Ivan, I think, and then a second one right behind it…that put this road under also….your bridge got washed away in that when I think a Volkswagen floated down and hit it and took the whole thing out after it took out the other bridge up the road. Then they built this one right after…but it took my barn that year, too. Nothing anyone could do. I didn't rebuild it since my husband and I broke up that next year and did not want to be bothered with a new project and had so many things to do already. My son does construction. I hear you are an architect." Amazingly there was no breadth taken yet, and I was wondering how she knew I was an architect. She continued, "I don't want to discourage you and be disappointed about what you're doing to the stream, but those rocks you're stacking won't do anything. You are just wasting your time. I applaud your energy but when the next heavy rain comes, they'll just be washed away. I know. I hear the boulders being tossed every rain behind my house. It looks pretty, but trust me, it will be gone."

Finally, a small pause. This happened not because she intended to stop talking or allow me to interject, but because she had to breathe. I told her, "I lost two birch trees from the erosion and was trying to help prevent any more damage."

She said, "I don't think the dams were built by people. They're just boulders getting washed down. I hear them every hard rain.

"Really," I said.

Bev continued, "But if it were me, I would just plant more trees further up the hill and not try to do anything else since it will just get washed out the next rain."

I said, "Good idea," although thinking that is the craziest and worst idea I had heard in a long time, it missed the point, and I assume she did not understand about the erosion but was all but willing to comment on the landscaping.

I said, "Thanks for stopping but I have to get back to work before the rain…."

She cut me off and went on, "You know nothing will work on this stream unless you dig out the center with a backhoe and completely rebuild the banks…they are supposed to do it at Cove Stream…."

They are already working on Cove Stream, I thought to myself, and I have my own thoughts on that.

"….I'd hate for you to waste your time…and those stones lining the edges won't do anything. I am the confessed neighborhood busy body," she said jokingly, "and I thought I'd stop by."

"Thanks, Bev, but I really need to get back to…."

"You know in '05 I was in the house and I heard those boulders being crashed downstream and thought the worst and then I heard a huge crash and my whole barn was washed down stream…maybe with that Volkswagen that hit your bridge…. Wayne rebuilt a good one and I like what you did to rebuild it."

I said, "Thank you and I need…."

She went on, "Wayne is living over at Cove Creek. I believe."

I jumped in quickly, "Yes, at the old mill I went there last week to say hello, you should stop by there Bev, today, I am sure he is there right now, and say hey. He would appreciate the company; he went out to New Mexico to see his squeeze and they got into a tiff and he and his sister drove back across country to Minnesota and then he bought her a house there and then he came back here. He's 82 now and going blind and drove across country to Minnesota then back here, but you should really stop by to see him. Well, I need to…."

Bev interjected, "Maybe I will. You know he did a lot of work on this place and got it looking good and he and his sister lived here for thirty years and rebuilt that bridge, did I tell you he built it after that back-to-back hurricane in '05 that took out my barn and road with it? None of us could get out and it took out the bridge next to the Hansens too. It washed it down stream. Maybe the barn and the Volkswagen took out the bridge? Then all of it took yours out. Well, gotta keep walking. Nice to talk to you. I live in the big white house up the road…just stopped to say hello to a new neighbor. Are you here by yourself and are you here full time? You know a lot of people don't live here full time but I have for thirty-four years and the Hansens have for forty years but a lot of folks have other homes, like in Charlotte and just come here to visit, but you are full time right but by yourself. That's what I heard."

I said, "Yes, just me…and my kids are in Kentucky, and they love this place. Thank you, Bev. I need to keep at it, but thanks for saying hello."

At that point I moved back down to the stream and started digging again hoping she got the message, and I honestly didn't know if she was still talking to me, but I needed to get back to work and before she might start again. Bev is harmless, a good neighbor and well intentioned, and I guess if she says so she is the self-proclaimed " neighborhood busybody," but Christ almighty! I needed to keep working. I thought "Planting the trees further up the hill?" Geez, what an insane idea. That statement equates to an old joke about the patient and doctor. The patient says, Doctor, my arm hurts when I do this. How do I stop the pain?"

Doctor says, "Don't do that."

Bev said goodbye again and this time proceeded with her walk down the gravel road.

When a terrible storm comes through the area with torrential rains there is nothing anyone can do in that case except ask the stream gods to be kind. That was an incredible occurrence with back-to-back hurricanes, Frances and Ivan, in '05. Bev had a point. If it happens again, yes, my work will be tested and who knows the outcome. But if completed it has a chance to survive. And I heartily appreciated the advice and the vote of confidence from the apparition in a pink coat.

Man in Motion
Painted Plaster Relief
Mark T. Wright

10-11-21

I have been too exhausted to write while working in the stream. Last week we had rain for five continuous days accumulating around six inches and the stream rose to a flooded level. Since the increased water volume was slow and incremental the layout, ideas and work held, and the stream reacted to the increased water level swimmingly. The stream showed me the direction she wanted to take and how she wanted to manage the excess water from the rain and runoff spread over several days. I had been trying to design and sculpt the stream to flow for low water levels and yet prepare for the high-water event, but it had not rained for weeks. The stream and I were finally tested. During these five days I studied the water and the current watching where the main current line flowed and where there were detrimental back currents causing over silting. Slight changes in the curvature and width of the bank edge placement allow a healthy water flow or a debacle and dead water. One rock changed upstream causes a ripple effect and a change in events downstream. One deeper hole placed, one drop, or one area widened modifies the intensity of the current at multiple levels shifting the action immediately upstream and down. So, the tuning of the stream must continue until we achieve balance.

The water was higher and, in some cases, to my mid-thigh which is wonderful...short lived but wonderful. The rain had subsided, and the trees were wet with darkened barks. The magnificence of standing in the water is that I am on the stream bottom, land, solid and strong as Antaeus with a watery plane flowing around me at my knee level. Above me there is a mystical tree canopy arching over the stream mimicking the stream bottom. Then the sky as another active living layer above that. It is a powerful feeling of breaking that surface plain with legs submerged, compressed, and pushed by the current, challenged slightly, caressed by the water playfully while the rest of my body is held by the air around me. I have the feeling of being sliced by the water surface plane but still solid on the earth, and at the same time being hugged by the tree canopy and kissed by the sky.

Suddenly, a strong October wind blew and as if on cue all the leaves from all the birch trees fell and danced in wonderful unison. Yellow and burned orange organic snowflakes floated down simultaneously in a migrating mass. But the wind would not let them all hit the stream. It carried a choice few, slowly in sway and drifting shimmering light as they danced a brilliant slow dance for me settling on the water and rocks over a period of seconds then resting and then repeating. Presumptuous, I know, but I believe they performed the enchanted dance for me to witness. In the mountains the leaves fall for a longer duration. A tree higher up the mountain sheds a leaf, and if lucky will fall from the highest elevation down to the stream area in a long beautiful slow twisting, flipping, floating, tumbling, shimmering, bending light around it, defying gravity then yielding to it; then fooling the laws for seconds, drifting, riding the wind then sliding above it, and shifting gracefully for a glorious, prolonged period. It is a simple unpredictable magical gift that slows time from what we are accustomed to. No two leaves will ever fall the same. Some will rest on the banks, the mountainsides, the flats, the gravel road, and some will land in the stream to take passengers on the magical downstream adventure explained by a nine-year-old blue-eyed general. Each trip is different.

At this point I am about seventy five percent successful at molding and preparing the stream for multiple situations, low water, and high water with a huge amount of work still to complete. I can see progress and happiness with the stream, the banks, the trees, the rocks, and the life there. The water temperature is below sixty degrees. The riffles and runs are working. The small deep holes are holding. The shift of the stream from the bank's edges to a center for water flow is occurring. The major meandering structure is adequate for about five hundred of the eight hundred feet of stream. The deeper center channels are beginning to appear. The next step is to shore up the banks with more stone and deepen the runs and channel and dig two more deep holes for fish to stay in summer and harsh winter and bad flooding. No more trees have been snatched from the bank soil by the terrible claws of that always ominous roaring dragon of a flooded stream, as they all seem to hold cautiously and gratefully, encouraged by the stones and boulders now hugging their roots.

I moved sixteen tons of rip rap to help stabilize a drainage ditch that feeds the stream. It worked and held through the flooding. The water, filtered by fifty-sevens, then rip rap in a small retention pool, bleeds into the stream. It has developed plants and grasses covering the area merging with the riparian area and it filters the runoff and sediment from the drainage before it reaches the stream. It has relieved the stream of the silt and mud that was flowing unabated into the stream at that point. By looks of that small area, I will need another fifty tons of rip rap stone to complete the work and help stabilize the banks along the stream. I have already moved more than sixty tons of stone by hand from the stream bed reviving and rerouting water to the center channel preventing water from eroding the banks.

Standing on the porch at the house, I am about eighty feet above the stream and with a pair of binoculars can see seventy-five percent of the stream from this vantage point. It is useful to step back, to capture the entirety of the work, as the mountain is clearer to the climber from a distance. Even from this elevated platform I cannot fully see the entire stream area but do gain a perspective on the overall connection from end to end and am able to recognize nuances that will better the work, as well as failures to repair.

While up at this perch, I saw four deer running across the yard. More like frolicked across the yard. They seemed happy to be out and relieved I was not bothering them causing a ruckus in the water. I saw a dark large shadow dart through the water up stream in one area for about twenty-five feet then stop and hold. It was a large trout which made me jubilant. I could not tell which kind of trout from this distance, but it was active and vibrant. While watching, a small mink popped his head up at the stream edge. Maybe interested in the trout. He looked around for a second then jumped into the rushing current and slinked under water effortlessly across the stream popping up and out and scurried up the bank and into the woods without missing a trick. These are simple gifts.

I anticipate it will take another year to massage the stream into shape to support fish. The work is sometimes overwhelming and arduous, and I did not fully realize the extent of the problems. So, I will continue to deliberately move one boulder and one shovel at a time repeatedly through the high water and low water. This translates to achieving depths of twelve to eighteen inches and a water temperature below sixty-eight degrees in the hottest months of the year, which coincides with the low water levels, usually July, August, and September. The water flow is finite, and I must anticipate the worst conditions of low water and try to also accommodate the damaging floods. A small task, (he said sarcastically) as I am amused at my attempts and my plan to bring her back. What else can I do?

10-21-21

The children came down last week and the moments were priceless. The time flew by like nothing I have ever experienced, yet when I list the things we did it allows me to be genuinely happy for short periods of time just embracing the mundane and the profound. The simple act of making cinnamon rolls from scratch with my son and him telling me he is limiting himself to two before we build sandcastles at the stream was an incredible show of self-restraint on his part. That is true willpower. Later that evening, we gathered firewood and stones to build a fire in the flat section of the yard directly below the South deck so we could roast marshmallows and make smores. They helped me with the wood and the stones. We all went earlier to get the goods for the smores. My thirteen-year-old daughter oversaw the smores process, I oversaw the fire, and my 8-year-old son oversaw entertainment.

I showed Harry how to build a fire by first placing the stones in a circle to contain the wood and ash. Then beginning with larger wood on the bottom and the tinder on top and my secret ingredient, dryer lint, as the helper. He lit the lint, and we watched as the tinder began to ignite, then the smaller sticks and then the larger twigs ignited, and finally the fire was holding itself alive. When the fire was ready Margaret Annie began to assemble the marshmallows on the thin limbs I found. I whittled each end to a point and free from bark as she sterilized them then with fire in preparation for the first step, the browning of the marshmallows. I write this with tears now. She, without provocation said, "I have Harry's set up so we can help him before we do ours." The kindest simplest thing. So, we waited for Harry to roast his marshmallow and she helped him make a smores showing him the secret when it was optimum timing to withdraw the roasted marshmallow and the perfect pinch between chocolate and graham cracker to squeeze it from the spit. Then she made hers as Harry crunched the morsel with delight. It is moments like this, where I am humbled and dumbfounded with delight by the innocent and beautiful kindness shown by my children, in a world that seems to have become increasingly mean and intolerant. But it makes me grateful. It gives me hope for the future.

Earlier in the day, between building sandcastles, Harry helped me work on part of the stream bank near the bridge. The little guy did not want to use any tool—he was simply happy doing the work with his hands. I gave him a pair of my rubber gloves to keep his hands warm and he worked hard. As he did this, I was in the stream shoveling out the silt that had built up over the forty years. Every shovel and every bit of work by Harry contributed and improved the stream flow. No contribution is too small if made with pure intent and with the best interest of the stream at heart. The back flow in this area began to reduce, the silt began to wash away, and the gravel bottom began to magically appear. The bank is becoming established and the whole width is becoming healthy.

10-25-21

Yesterday, in the upper stream section, I stood overwhelmed with the amount of work left to accomplish. But again, with every small clearing of debris and breaking of dams and clearing paths, the stream reacts positively, and I know I must be patient in the work. So much of the work involves silent moments where I must stop and evaluate the water immediately by studying the time, the direction, the dispersion, and the depth that the suspended particles that I stir take. This reading of the water is paramount to assess what the stream wants to become and where we can compromise as partners to achieve balance. In the end she and the water will win any argument. A hard rain or a long absence of rain informs me of my mistakes, failed assumptions and small false successes. For these imposters only affect my ego and the only vital measure is life thriving in the stream family.

Standing solemn in the stream, the butterfly effect is the most obvious. One minor change upstream affects the movement, flow, and action downstream. It is a brilliant microcosm and metaphor for our global environment. And globally, as I see it, one heat wave in England, the ongoing drought in Kenya, the ice sheet melting in Greenland, affects the water in this stream; the rain feeding it; the salamanders in it; the hummingbirds above it—they all affect each other and us. But that is the beauty and joy of it all—the universal non exclusivity. The stream is part of a living and active project that will take years to re-establish to a tentative balance. And all I am doing is trying to repair the damage.

I began work on the stream after it had evolved to this current "evolved form;" however unhealthy and out of balance. A wide flat flooding form and extreme erosion and undercutting of the banks may not have happened here unless there was careless altering of the land. Upstream and downstream the banks are higher and steeper and deep and lined with boulders.

Once the stream crosses over the property line upstream, it is obvious the change in the topology that caused a widened flat shift in the stream form. The stream edges undercut are causing the beautiful birch trees to fall. The area under the bridge is flat and widened. The areas beside the bridge where there was once earth is now barren and worn. The gradually sloping banks are not necessarily a terrible thing in and of themselves, but they need to be carefully integrated into the stream topography to be effective during flooding.

The finite amount of water normal in the stream cannot support a healthy ecosystem when the center bed is aggregated and raised and widened without a center channel. The water was barely flowing and was one half inch deep. This increase in surface area caused the water temperature and accelerated evaporation to rise in the dry hot summer months, and this in turn caused less water flowing in the stream. There were no deeper sections and no riffles to oxygenate the water. Without a main deeper channel, the stream would immediately flood wider to the edges when heavy rains came. This caused more erosion and more silting in the stream. Then the pendulum swings back to flat wide shallow warmer flows of water. In the one deep section, near the bridge, the silt buildup compounded itself to cause increased filling of the bottom, shifting the water flow and causing a major backflow and the cycle continued. This silt closed the channel, raised the bottom area and narrowed the habitable area for life. Coupled with multiple dams built, the environment was a vicious fabricated mess. This was not the stream chasing a natural evolution of form. It is the stream reacting to our intrusions.

It has not rained in five days, and I observed the areas still suffering slow or low water flow. However, because of the work, there is water flowing in all parts of the stream now where none existed before the work began. I worked on an area that had a gathering of natural boulders all of which were bound up with debris, silt, and leaves. They are magnificent in their random stations and brilliant in their stubborn nature. I am compelled to release some of them and let them breathe again. They were speaking to me as the masculine piece of this stream, formed over thousands of years by the caress of the water, yet resilient in their resistance to her. I do not know if they have always been here covered by hundreds of years of memories or if they were rolled and tossed into position by the water recently. But they found me, and I heard their call to action.

A 3,000 pound boulder eight-feet diameter teetered on a small rock ledge. It spontaneously fell from the upper bank and permanently altered the stream.

The larger boulders can resist the rush of the stream, unlike the smaller rocks that appear to be childlike free spirits in the stream, tumbled by the push of the water starting upstream, ending downstream, and seeming unconcerned where they land. We see them spread along the bottom in lesser currents, huddled together making the mosaic gravel bottom waiting for an uptick in water velocity to jostle them to life, moving them again, until they accumulate on the upstream side as piranhas devouring their prey against an unperturbed steadfast boulder. However, with resistance comes a price. Those larger boulders, in their stubbornness, are sometimes covered like dinosaur bones by silt and smaller rocks. Their resistance is not their total demise, but their slow waltz to obscurity. Where once they stood proud and steadfast in defiance, they are now buried in the silt and smaller rocks that they resisted. Only the well placed bolder in a healthy stream environment allows the water to pass around it, kissing it gently, with stream and rock content in its symbiotic relationship; boulder slowing stream smoothed and refined, and the stream embracing boulder but continuing to feed and nurture the downstream environment.

After surveying the remaining work yesterday, I had moments of overwhelming stupor thinking that even the mighty Hercules may second guess attempting this huge task at hand and would prefer, instead, cleaning the Augean stables. I was wearing insulated boots instead of waders, and water slowly snuck into both after a few hours. The water temperature is now below fifty degrees, and even with thick wool socks my damp feet could not retain warmth. My hands are beginning to feel the dropping colder temperatures and are stiffening, and I will not be able to work there for many more days. I painstakingly study each area so as not to harm the natural water flow with the work but always attempt to enhance it.

While I was silently contemplating my next steps, my friend a damselfly came again to see my work. She sadly has only a few ticks of the clock left to explore this year before it is too cold for her, and she will not know winter. Innocently and romantically, I would like to think she is the same one I see with every visit to the stream. I interpret her presence as reassurance that what I am doing is of no harm and is improving her habitat. She seems happy with the work, and I hope it is a sign that what I am doing is not in vain. Technically, I know she is a predator, and I am stirring up aquatic insects and she is like the blackbirds in a corn field at harvest time waiting to pick off grasshoppers. The farmer on the tractor harvests the crops, stirs up the grasshoppers and the blackbirds come to feast, but at the same time to say thank you to the farmer. I take pleasure in entertaining the idea that she is here to do both. I see her existence as a magical colorful flying pot of gold at the end of the rainbow, and not simply the refraction of white light through a prism as defined by entomology.

The trumpet vine has stopped flowering, and I have not seen the hummingbirds for a week now and assume they are heading south to prepare for their trip across the Gulf of Mexico.

10-28-21

The weather is changing. We experience here in the mountains, the exaggerated and extreme swings reflected across the country. Average temperatures are higher in the evenings and the mountains struggle to cool the air. The stream is feeling the unyielding pressure and yet it continues. Every house, every road, every driveway added over the last one hundred years adds to the runoff and heat displacement and the changes in the stream. These structures will not go away and are now a permanent part of the system, with some to be added in the future. Who can say to what extent we have permanently altered this environment, but the impacts of our actions are undeniable. We have incrementally invaded the natural boundaries of the stream with obvious impacts, maybe innocently seeking quiet solace in nature, clean air, et cetera; but we have, with somewhat blatant disregard, built structures adding to the impervious surface while removing pervious surfaces that filter and slow the runoff to the stream.

Extreme weather conditions are becoming prevalent from warmer winters, warmer nights and instead of normal rains gracing the streams and rivers, we have extreme events creating floods. The rising temperatures and saturated soil drive crawdads from their underground lairs earlier. Daffodils are punching through the ground in February. The data shows average nights are warmer and the people living in these mountains for forty years can testify to this reality. Houses never needing air conditioning in these mountains now require it in summer. The last ten years have yielded less snow and warmer and wetter winters. Hummingbirds stay longer because flowers bloom longer. There are less amounts of snow at one time, less snow staying over time, less dry fluffy soft snow accumulating being replaced with wet heavy icy snow due to warmer temperatures. The local ski resorts must make more snow and plan for warmer temperatures.

This is not a disease exclusive to the mountains of North Carolina. I spoke to a young man on a plane traveling for work to the US from Brussels, Belgium who expressed the same concerns and observations. The changes there, with drier hotter summer months, are drying up the canals and have caused an economic burden restricting and stopping the water traffic. The winters are warmer, and the canals do not freeze in the winter, so they haven't ice skated on the canals in five years. To take drastic action and stop any further harm to the environment, Belgium has placed a moratorium, a 'building shift' and a goal to halt all new buildings in the country by 2040. The only permitted action is renovations, or the tearing down of existing buildings and building back new structures. Likewise, temperatures are increasing in the United States, and they feel it in cities in the west such as Phoenix, AZ. Nights are not cooling, so evaporation is rampant and the problem with lack of water is a huge issue. These are but a few examples. Did they affect this small stream, or did we contribute to their problems, or have we all contributed at a micro and macro level and affect and infect each other? I believe the latter. The butterfly effect.

Those that deny the undeniable and say the events are cyclical and natural, I cannot waste one precious breadth trying to argue rationally against their irrationality. They need only live in these mountains, walk in the stream, and breathe the air; then talk to the people who have witnessed the changes. Even the people who live here may not admit they had a hand in the indiscretions resulting in the change, but they will not deny the changes. If it is cyclical, we are at the beginning of a new cycle not yet reaching the pinnacle of the arch.

I am a planner and an incrementalist at heart and believe, regardless of the causes, the effects resulting from global warming are real, happening in real time, and are felt with obvious repercussions. We cannot un-ring the horrific bell of damage we have already rung, but we can soften the clanging and come to hear an eventual gentle ping. Make no mistake, the planet will continue to live on despite us, just as the stream will continue to heal itself or continue to exist in horrific extremes, finally resulting in completely dry channels and extreme flooding. We may push ourselves into extinction, but the planet will regroup and recover from our transgressions after we are gone. I prefer to attempt taking on the tall task of proving to the stream and land that I am a worthy partner, taking what I have learned, and what I offer as recompense to help heal us all. I may not succeed completely by the time my sun sets, but the seeds will have been planted for my children to cultivate, and I need to know I leave a legacy of effort.

The main stream structure in place is beginning to transform the new channel increasing water flow, and now the depths need tweaking, adding to the diversity in bottom structure. Now with an established meandering center channel, the stream has a normal water flow continuously and can reach its flood plain when flood flows surpass the bank fill stage. This should also help transfer silt away and help maintain constant water levels in summer. The increase in depth and flow reduces the stream's chances of freezing over and it will also help provide fish with a safe holding spot. I have underestimated the amount of fill and rip rap needed to fill the bank's sides. I am guessing that it might take sixty tons of rip rap to bring up the levels on the east side and another twenty tons for the west side.

However, I will continue with the plan, clear the center stream channel, and use that material to fill in the bank edges before I order the stone. It may surprise me, but I am skeptical that I can gather all the material I need from the center to complete the edge work.

Subtle moves such as lifting a bottom rock but not taking it out of the stream bottom can make a beautiful difference in the flow and oxygen added to the stream. Executing all work by hand is exhausting and time consuming. But doing so I can experience the subtleties like witnessing a salamander skidding from under a rock and sliding between three rocks as it contorts its body to hide. It is an amazing gift and a sign that lets me know the water is cleaner and oxygenated because of the work. Crayfish are moving continuously, and small fish emerge from the cover I created. Hopefully, I am helping improve the environment assisted by clues suggested by the stream when it's resting and moving slowly; where it is excited and moving steadily; where it is anxious and moving rapidly; and where it is desperate and flooding. I choose to take the narrow beautiful view that measures my success with one question: is life returning and maintaining in the stream environment. I have no other measures of substance. I have insignificant benchmarks and celebrate small victories with the miraculous sound of the water moving and the wonderful aesthetic of the meandering stream. These constant celebrations help me continue. But life, seeing life in abundance again, pervading these waters is the only significant measure.

Harry shoveling gravel from the bottom of the stream.

Chapter X

10-30-21

It rained buckets again the last three days and the stream flooded but returned to balance quickly. I am sure Bev was surprised. It maintained the structure, overflowed the banks as expected, and the places I had not addressed flooded disastrously, violently, sadly, and now I have a plan for those areas. The structure and general plan are sufficient, but the details are fluid and ever changing. My research and examination of academic papers and case studies have been instrumental, but the time in the water is irreplaceable. General solutions work, but this small stream is a textbook example filled with every warning sign you can imagine associated with a stream out of balance. Warning signs such as braided channels, a nonexistent main center channel, mid channel bars of excessive sediment, widened banks evolved to absorb the increased discharge energy during flood events causing erosion and undercutting, are a few of the problems. So, the solutions to bring this stream to balance, in partnership with the elements, require a patient search for the correct combination of solutions and techniques merging into a hybrid over time in this small area. It is not a fight or reconstruction, but a beautiful slow dance where I sometimes lead and sometimes follow.

But the theories and applications are solid if we execute them in varied combinations. I tried diverters in areas for an experiment and they worked for a brief time. I tried the hook diverters in cases, and they worked in a limited capacity. The issue is that the water flow of the stream is inconsistent and limited, and in some cases the diverter caused problems, or were ineffective all together. The most effective measures to bring the stream to balance, after working in the stream for over 3,000 hours so far, appear to be altering the form of the stream to a subtle meandering shape and varying the depth and narrowing the width. By this I mean, instead of it being a straight run of water as the stream has become, with a crown in the middle, create a curved and meandering shape with diverse water action. This slows the water energy in flood conditions and varies the speed of flow and increases oxygen in the water. Boulders help, but the depth will be the answer along with the meandering shape. This is not a simple two-dimensional form as shown on a site plan, a topographic map, or an aerial view. It is not simply a three-dimensional form expressed in depth width and length that falls from the highest elevation to the confluence of the river via gravity. It is not simply a fourth dimensional form expressing itself over time; it is a changing, wondering, chaotic living vibrating multidimensional spiritual entity.

We do know some simple, perhaps obviously basic magical and unifying things from working and observing this phenomenon, the stream. At the simplest level, moving water erodes. Sometimes we can use this as a positive advantage. The faster the current the more vigorous the water erodes. Even if we do not perceive the effect in our real time it is happening in stream time. Water is the blood of the stream veins and carries the nutrients for the stream life. The more oxygen in the water the stronger the life. The more nutrients the more life. Gravity is the generator. There is no heart pump returning water through a closed loop as with our own human body. The only loop is the huge environmental water cycle. An open loop for the stream. This open loop exposes the water to outside factors such as evaporation and temperature swings. We know that deeper areas develop after a waterfall regardless of the scale and oxygenates this water at the same time. We know the outside edge of the "S" shape on the stream will erode and be the deeper section with greater current speed. We know that squeezing the stream sides and bottom increases the water speed at the area, thus increasing erosion. This is simple compression, and the reciprocal is the expansion of the stream which causes slower water and less erosion. As with the fable about the smart crow wanting a drink of water, displacement raises water levels so it's reciprocal lowers the water levels.

Deep holes will develop immediately after a waterfall and fast narrowed runs from good erosion. This will help wash out the silt and oxygenate the deeper hole. Also, at these points I want to create deeper areas for fish to survive winter freezes and higher summer temperatures. This will all vary of course in flood situations and in drought conditions. It can never be perfect, but I am trying to achieve continuous controlled water flow in the worst conditions possible in a small area.

Carl Freeman stopped by yesterday, and he is getting his hip replaced this week. He has been a resident of these mountains for fifty years, a fly-fishing guide and a friend. He is a Vietnam veteran and cancer survivor. Now widowed, his wife fell prey to complications from the COVID-19 virus. Carl is one of those people who everyone loves: personable, always ready with a story, always in a hurry running from his shadow and his footprints; hilarious and a walking caricature of himself; harmless and good natured, with a contagious smile he can shift on a dime to make clients feel comfortable.

He pulled up unannounced, in his Ford F250 red truck, topper on the bed, with his logo for fly fishing and clay shooting trips painted on both side panels, rigged for fly fishing and clay pigeon shooting trips, and his beautiful brown lab named Moo in the front passenger seat. He parked at the lower section of the property just beyond the bridge. I saw him cross the bridge and went up from the stream to meet him. He is a small, white bearded, thin man with gold rimmed glasses who looks like a mini- Santa Claus, full of local fishing knowledge and many tall tales. He wore a long-sleeved dress shirt, clean well pressed jeans, and perfectly shined cowboy boots. He was not going fishing or heading to the gun range.

"Hey brother," he said with his head slightly pushed out of the rolled down window and his elbow on the door as he pulled up. "How's it hangin' butter bean? I was up in Banner Elk picking up shells for the clay shooting. Hell, I can't find them anywhere right now but a fella there had what I needed. I've been so busy with the clay shooting I have about four minutes to say hey and wanted to see how the stream was coming."

He slowly twisted out of his truck obviously in pain as he swiveled his leg around to the left and down on the running board followed gingerly by his right leg, waited a moment, then still hanging onto the grip mount handle above his head slowly lowered himself down. As soon as he was out Moo took off searching, sniffing tracking, and stretching.

"Man, it looks gooood. Moo," he whistled. "Moo, here boy."

"Good to see you, man, how's the fly-fishing guiding?" I asked.

"I have been so busy with the clays; I have a couple other guides I hired to do the fly fishing. Besides those rocks are slicker than a cat's ass and I have to get my hip worked on this week but, man, this really looks good and you're doing it right." He said, and I still have no idea what that reference is supposed to mean even after twelve years of fishing with him, but the rocks are slick.

"I'm trying my friend, and Moo is beautiful," I said.

He lowered his voice and stretched out the words. "Yeah, the stream looks so good, you're doing it right, can't wait to see it when you're done and fish are coming back...Moo....man he's such a great dog," he whistled again.... "Well, I gotta go, meeting a group at the diner and going to shoot clays tomorrow then on Friday going to Raleigh to get my hip worked on. I'll keep you posted. Later gator.... Here Moo."

He whistled again and Moo came quickly, jumped into the truck on the driver's side and scooted across, and Carl climbed in the same deliberate slow painful way he got out and then drove away. He mentioned that trout migrate, and I said, "Hell Carl, all trout migrate, it is in their blood, it is ancient instinct, Carl."

The stream and the rocks too still have ancient energy since it is not fabricated. Every boulder speaks to me and I to the stream. Each stone has its own life and activity inherent and attached to it. The same boulder placed in the stream cannot be placed in the same spot in the same position twice, therefore the dynamic action it introduces is unique every time and the random action of the water acting on the stone changes over time effecting the stone and thus changing the water.

This is the chaotic brilliant interaction that no equation can predict. I ask: is the energy of the water changing the stone and taking microscopic particles from it, or is the stone giving itself voluntarily, sacrificially, and shrinking incrementally to the water eventually knowing after millennia it will disappear, merging with the water to immediately change her composition? We can see this action accelerated in real time if we watch the bottom silt being carried away exposing the pebbled, then stone, then bedrock bottom of the stream. We can see this happen to pieces of glass that fall into the stream, jagged and clear at the beginning becoming beautifully opaque and smooth over time.

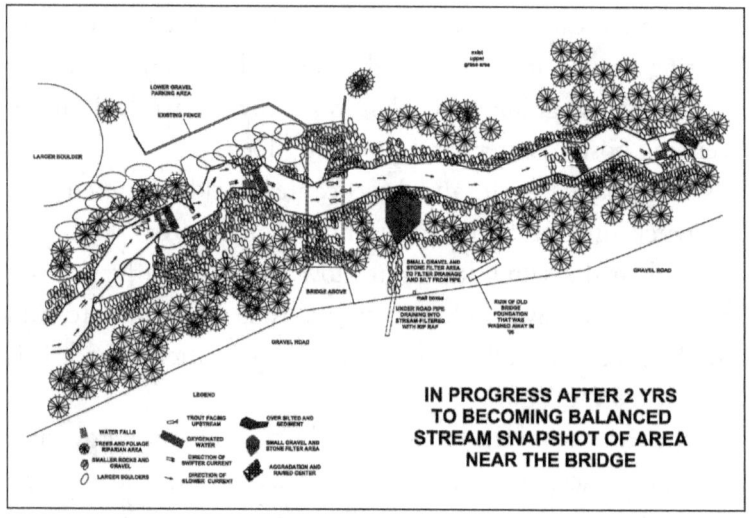

Millions of years ago a sharp boulder resting in the stream and formed by the moving water, over time, became a smoothly shaped entity holding countless memories of the stream life and the water. I would like to believe, the stone desired to be smooth, giving its jagged edges to the stream, microscopic particle by particle, in exchange for the glorious experiences in the water over time. As it resisted the water it changed the course of the stream creating brilliant complex energies. It added gritty contributions to the water along with that of other stones, and it has been carried in solution for millennia, to mold other rocks. The contradiction is that as the stone becomes smoother and smaller its memory of stream life events increases and its energy of recollections become denser. But selflessly the stone releases its energy back into the stream. Water and particles of stone dance downstream together continuously repeating the poetry.

Standing in the stream, looking as I have since I began this journey, I'll find existing boulders imbedded in the bedrock, sometimes 4, 6, 8, 10, 12 feet in diameter, in the stream that have no desire to move. The stream and the water know the complex interrelationship between these boulders that may have existed since time began and they are coaxing me to search for those relationships and advance them to mold the new direction and meandering shape of the stream. The clues are there like line drawings by numbers, connecting channel and stream edges, holding water; and all we need to do is take the time to look, use our imagination and let our mind float free to see how the water could move around these existing boulders as it may have done since time began. Again, they exist steadfast in the stream and can be used as anchors holding and supporting other smaller boulders and rocks. There is a relationship that exists between these boulders; multiple relationships, complex relationships, sometimes obvious, other times hidden. I study a stretch of stream long enough and find the existing relationships and augment them to help bring the stream back to balance. And as the stream form changes, so does the complexity of each existing stone. A group of boulders may act as a team in concert to change water flow and direction. Two boulders placed or found close together accelerate water between them. It is like the water is playing a game and must hurry past the two stones, or it is late to the party downstream.

11-2-21

It was Halloween in the stream. I miss the children most at these times and dreamed fantasized discussions with Harry and Margaret Annie asking questions if, the salamanders would dress up like Toothless in *How to Train Your Dragon*, the crawdads as Russian bakers in *The Nutcracker*, if the muskrat would be Mr. Busy in *Lady and the Tramp*, the blue heron as Foghorn Leghorn, and the mink as Rudyard Kipling's *Rikki-Tikki-Tavi*. Harry is so excited about his scarecrow costume, and Margaret Annie dressed as a beautiful witch is getting too old for the routine but still loves the candy. As I was standing there, the neighborhood dog came trotting by, free, unencumbered, with his attitude of pure delightful independence. He has an owner, somewhere, but is simply charming and friendly to anyone while spreading his own type of mountain welcoming. I can't help but stop, smile, and say hello, but only for a brief moment, as he has places to go and others to meet.

Yesterday was All Saints' Day and today is All Souls' Day. As the adults did when I was a child, they would be celebrating; and if by a stream, evoking St. Florian as the patron saint against floods, and St. Christopher (even though he is no longer a member of the club) for the safe travels, and St. Francis, patron saint of the animals. Then on All Souls' Day , we remember the souls of those lost and who have left their bodies on this planet. There also exists a mystical, magical energy in the stream that must be partially due to the eons of life and the souls that stepped foot and feet here, from the smallest of animals to man. But the water evokes a beautiful mythical childhood story and metaphor for perseverance and carrying the weight of our life's events on our shoulders while showing a simple act of kindness; it is the story of St. Christopher's determination and dedication to the task of carrying the child across the river.

One day St. Christopher, who was a large strong man whose kindness and dedication to God was expressed by his dedication helping travelers cross a dangerous river, was standing by the water's edge when a small child came to the stream and was going to cross. St. Christopher knowing the water was too deep and too strong for the child to cross, offered to carry the boy on his shoulder. As he was carrying the lad, the weight of the boy grew heavier and heavier with every step across the river. St. Christopher asked the boy why he grew so heavy. The boy replied that he was the Christ child and that he was burdened with the weight of all the sins of the world. Determined not to give up, St. Christopher made it across. The lad thanked St. Christopher by turning his staff into a tree along the banks edge.

The leaves are almost completely shed by the trees, the temperature is falling, and the winds are biting at us much harder. There are a few stubborn Red Maple trees refusing to comply with the notice to evacuate their cover. Although it is sad to lose the foliage, the benefit is I can see more of the stream exposed through the naked tree canopy from the porch with binoculars. In the other seasons more of the view is obscured in several areas by the foliage. This is a wonderful daily surprise as each fall dawn pulls back the leaf curtains uncovering a broader vista of the stream.

It snowed slightly, chilling the stream and making it difficult to work in the water except for short periods. On to the inside of the house to work for a while until the day re-warms enough for me to return to the water. There will be intermittent warmer days allowing me to work. Although the water temperature is below fifty degrees the air temperature, when above forty degrees Fahrenheit makes it tolerable to work in the stream when dressed appropriately. I think of an interesting phenomenon existing on some winter days. Generally, the flowing stream water maintains a temperature of thirty-two degrees Fahrenheit, which on some days can be warmer than the air temperature. There is a scientific explanation, but I think it's stream magic.

11-15-21

It happens mostly in the summertime; however, people are still coming to the area at this time of year, and I'm constantly asked while working on the stream, "How do we get to the falls?" I stop and try to assist them, detailing the trek and attempting to coach them on the danger, the difficulty, the ease, and beauty of the falls. I'll let them know if they go on upstream behind the falls there is a visual treasure for the senses hidden, often overlooked. Often, I see people walking up the stream onto the property searching for the same falls. I'm always perplexed and wonder where they searched and started in the stream, but I am cordial, and I guide them out and up and direct them to the falls.

I found three young men trespassing, walking in the stream and destroying areas I had built, building dams, and stacking boulders, rearranging the deflectors, and moving rocks indiscriminately. They had total disregard for the property and the stream and took it upon themselves to damage the work without reason except their own ignorance. There is half a mile of stream below me and over two miles of stream above me that I do not control. I only control 800 feet of stream where it crosses onto my property, and they chose this area to rampage for some unknown reason. I have signs posted along my section of the property and the road and in the stream showing that this is private property.

"Gentlemen this is private property," I shouted so they could hear above the sound of the falls. "Gentlemen," I said again since they appeared not to hear me. They continued damming the stream at the bridge. I walked closer.

"Hey bro," one of the gentlemen said.

I said, "Hey bro, this is private property and please stop moving the rocks."

"We're just building a dam," another one said. "We didn't know."

"I know what you are doing, so please leave now. Didn't you see the signs?"

"Yeah, bro, we saw the signs, but we didn't think." He mumbled something I did not understand as he stood directly under one of the signs.

I said, "And bro, so you saw the signs and you still came on here. What do you think those signs mean? The stones are there for reason. So please leave. Get out of the stream and walk back on the road."

They complied and as they were leaving said something to the effect of, "I'm with ya' bro."

The strong scent of marijuana lingered in the air under the bridge and followed them up the bank to the road. They may be OK young men, but they did not care where they put the rocks.

Harry and I relocating a small fish into a new habitat.

Chapter XI

11-28-21

The children came down for Thanksgiving, the first one we celebrated at the mountain house, and it is the beginning of a new tradition. It was a wonderful weekend where we hiked Grandfather Mountain for the first time, and it was a thrill for the children to run across the swinging bridge over the top the gorge which was at 6,000 feet above sea level. We parked at the second highest parking level and hiked to the top of the mountain and the swinging bridge. After hiking back down and driving back to the house, later we hiked down the gravel road and crossed the highway, climbed down the mountainside to the Watauga River then back under the highway tunnel to begin our hike at the bottom of the waterfall. We then hiked up to the waterfall, climbed over the top of the last boulder at the waterfall and hiked the entire stream back to the house. The next day we all hiked, climbed since there were no trails, up the back mountain just to see what was at the top. Harry was particularly excited by this and ran up the side of that mountain just like a small mountain goat. We reached the first plateau atop the mountain and arrived at a beautiful flat area filled with mountain pine trees. Later that evening we all gathered stones and wood for a campfire that we planned to have after we went fishing.

On Thanksgiving Day by popular demand and request we had chicken tenders, French fries, and pizza, leftover Indian food, and I insisted on at least one vegetable; so we did have broccoli for Thanksgiving dinner. On Friday we went fishing at a private stream for huge trout. The weather was beautiful but still a little crisp, and the temperature was around sixty degrees for the high that day. Harry had not yet mastered the art of casting and I wanted to make sure that he was going to catch nice fish; therefore I would cast for him, and as soon as we hooked a fish I would hand him the rod and reel so that he would bring the fish into the net. While I was casting to part of the stream next to a bunch of small rhododendrons, Margaret Annie and the guide who were just upstream for me began to yell and raise their hands. I turned quickly and realized that Harry had fallen.

Although the air temperature was not that cold the water temperature was fifty degrees. Water filled his little waders, so his pants became soaked and his legs and feet cold. He has a slight problem with staying warm in chilly weather so we immediately dropped everything, ran up the side of the bank, got him back to the truck, took off the waders, dried him out, and let him sit for a minute so he could get warm. The sun was out, and the inside of the truck was as toasty as a greenhouse and ready to help warm him. Margaret Annie never missed a trick and kept fishing like a trooper. Harry's pride was a little hurt and the spring taken out of his step so I let him sit for a little while with a blanket so that he could warm up. I told him everyone falls. It is part of the initiation into the club. "Did you fall, Papa?" he asked.

"Harry," I said in a matter of fact, deliberate delivery, "I fell one time in December when the temperature was about forty degrees. I just hooked a gigantic fish and was standing in two feet of water, and I got my foot caught between two rocks. I had the rod high in the air and fell straight backwards and went completely underwater. My hat flew off and floated downstream. As I was flat out and underwater, I took a quick accounting to see if I had broken anything and Carl, who was with me that day, said I had snapped back up like one of those clown punching bags with its bottom filled with sand. I still had the rod in my hand and the fish was still on. Carl grabbed my hat, gave it back to me and we landed the fish. I was freezing cold but did not stop fishing!"

He laughed and I could tell he was warming up and feeling better. I convinced him to come back down, and I had an idea where he would not have to get back into the water but could still catch fish. I surveyed the side of the stream and thought I could get Harry to come down and catch fish if I hooked the fish and brought the rod to him while he's standing dry on the side of the stream. He put on his jacket and his vest and came back down to the stream with us, and I told him how we would catch fish even if he didn't get in the stream and he would stay completely dry. So, on we went, I cast hooked then handed the rod to Harry for him to land a fish. Shortly thereafter, Harry and I hooked a brown trout the guides called "Bad, Bad Leroy Brown." He is a 34-inch-long brown trout. I set the hook and immediately handed the rod to Harry. The huge fish broke water and jumped, and Harry fought him for about 2 minutes, and I thought the fish was going to pull Harry into the stream like a whale pulling a dingy, but I also thought he was going to land this behemoth, before Leroy broke his line. This is a tough fish to land for the most experienced angler, but Harry gave it a go. Margaret Annie just did her usual spectacular best. She is beautiful to watch on the water and is a natural at all parts of flyfishing from casting to landing the fish. She is patient and determined and takes instructions wonderfully and executes them with grace. She caught a twenty-eight-inch rainbow trout completely on her own, from casting to hookset to landing the beast, and the entire process was a textbook example of the best of flyfishing and wonderful to watch.

We later had hot showers, hot chocolate under warm blankets, and an early dinner since we all were hungry after the wonderful day of fishing. Later we built a campfire, listened to the stream, told more stories of my falls, and slips in the stream, retold the stories of each fish caught today, and ate way too many smores. In all we caught twenty fish over twenty inches; a great day for any angler, and we caught fish most anglers dream of catching in their lifetime. These children were beautiful on the water and had reverence for these gorgeous animals and handled each with care. When netting these fish, we try not to take them out of the water to release them, except occasionally to get a photograph. After the first two fish that each of them caught, they both wanted to leave every other fish caught in the water so as not to take a chance on hurting the trout. These two small, beautiful souls understand.

Saturday, we went into town quickly for ornaments to decorate the Christmas tree. This was the start of a new tradition in the mountains. My job was to assemble the tree, make sure the lights work, and put the initial tinsel around the tree before I turned it loose for the kids to place all the ornaments. They did a splendid job and Margaret Annie took a slow-motion photograph of all the work so we would have it for posterity. The most important ornament was Harry's favorite 'taco' that

I placed in a position of honor atop the tree substituting for the star. We then had a quick dinner and then we watched the *Doctor Strange* Marvel movie while snuggled on the couch.

The entire weekend brought back memories when I was Harry's age and the house on 18th St. burned. There were nine of us living there and a fire happened in the afternoon while we were all at school, and everyone except Nannie, my great grandmother, was not home. The Catholic school was only two blocks from the house and that day my Aunt Sis came to the crossing guard after school and my brother, and I thought it was strange. She waited across the street for us. We were happy to see her because she was always great fun and a little crazy. She was my grandmother's cousin.

Her mother was Nannie's sister Maggie. Maggie married Will and lived just across the street from the house on 18th street. Every night after we had dinner, Nannie made Maggie and Will plates of food that I would take across the street and up the hill to them. Once a week my Aunt Sis came and picked up my brother and me in her Cadillac. She pulled around the block across the street and down the back alley behind Maggie's house. My brother and I waited in the car until she told us the coast was clear. Then we got out quickly as she opened the trunk and there were always three cases of beer in bottles. We were to grab the cases of beer and run discreetly up the steps to the back door. He was a retired blacksmith for the L and N railroad, and he still had arms like Popeye from the years of work. Maggie made him breakfast at 6:00 a.m., same thing every day: two eggs, bacon. and toast. It would sit sometimes until noon if he were not hungry. After the delivery, we would wait for the signal and carry down the weeks' worth of cases of empty bottles and load them back in the trunk. Aunt Sis gave us each a dollar for the work.

She met us and said, "Your house burned." I laughed because she was always kidding us, although I thought this was a little extreme and it was unusual, she was meeting us after school. She said, "Mark, no, your house burned."

I remember an inexplicable panic as I took off running home and the only thing, I could think about was, "Is Nannie OK?" I reached the house and standing there in the front yard was my mother with her cousin Big Donnie, and the firefighters were just finishing. Nannie was next door, and no one was in the house. Everyone was safe. After I knew Nannie was safe, funny things run through your head in moment like this. The weather was unusually warm for November and my brother, and I were wearing identical hand me down sweaters we received from the next-door neighbors who had older boys. Mom had just picked up our winter coats from layaway at JC Penney's. Mine was a blue plaid coat and my brothers was a green plaid coat. But both were gone in the fire, and I saw remnants of each of them in the front yard burned and wet. So, we had the clothes on our backs.

There were nine people living in the house, everyone was safe, but we all were homeless. Never think, kindness shown by you will not return to you. Aunt Sis and her husband, Art, let most of us stay in her semi-finished basement, so we had a place to live. So, Nannie, my grandmother (both grandfathers were dead by then), my mother, brother and sister took up residence in the basement. We put up blankets hung on clotheslines for the walls and slept on cots and rollaway beds. We all celebrated my birthday and Thanksgiving there in her basement. But it was the best Thanksgiving for all of us since we were safe, and we all survived the fire. Material items were just things and were replaceable, but we were all alive and together. Ironically, I had many Thanksgivings with the family and the children, and

I felt like that Thanksgiving after the fire was the best I ever had until this one with the children in the mountains.

They innocently lit up the high country and this house with their brilliant energy that I selfishly absorbed. I took them back on Sunday to meet their mother halfway between Kentucky and North Carolina and then drove three hours back to the mountains. It was a long melancholic trip packed with many memories to spare. I arrived home just before dark and stopped at the lower parking area of the house next to the bridge. I slowly stretched out of the car and stood on the bridge for a few moments seeing, smelling, hearing, and feeling the stream saying, "Welcome home my friend!" I drove on up the mountain, parked, and went into the house, empty but still ringing with the voices of the children and holding their energy seen in the lit Christmas tree. I had leftovers for dinner, started cleaning up, started laundry, read a bit then went to sleep to the sound of the stream and in the warm cradle of the beautiful moments my children had given me.

Then came Monday morning, and I could barely get out of bed, and I had severe chills and a headache. They began about 9:00 a.m. and lasted until 9:00 p.m. Nothing I could do relieved me, and I shivered for twelve hours as I lay on the couch fading in and out of sleep. I tried to sleep that night but then came the severe congestion and muscle pain and fatigue on Tuesday. My real estate agent, Traci Artus, who has become a good friend, called and heard I was sick.

Traci is a tall slim, sophisticated woman who dresses in the perfect English country attire as if she walked straight out of the *Garden and Gun* magazine advertisement for Barbour or Ralph Lauren. I am assuming this is a result of her long stays in England and New York. She is one of the best real estate agents I have ever known. She is caught between the business of real estate and the beauty of these mountains—reflecting her upbringing. She is patient, but not accepting of any false people. She worked tirelessly representing me, and one evening said in her cigarette smoking deepened feminine voice, "OK, I have this house, it's a little far out but it's for sale with a potential to buy the adjacent cottage and another piece of land. There's a stream along the property." We had looked at one hundred properties over a year and I am sure she was convinced that I could never be satisfied, as opposed to simply being a discerning buyer. "Sure," I said, "I'll meet you there. Text me the address."

Photograph by Wayne Lazorik

We met and she had a real estate agent's sword and shield in tow, hell bent for leather on protecting me from dragons of the sellers. But it was the home I had been looking for and I made an offer for the house, cottage, and the extra parcel. I felt a kinship with the older owner Wayne and made the offer with the typical contingencies, plus one. That Wayne allows me twelve hours of visits and one piece of photography he took from his collection. He agreed. And we met and he told me stories of his life and work and the history of the house. And they are now my stories.

Traci came by with an arsenal of cold remedy products plus a COVID-19 test she left on the side porch next to a container of chicken soup. Wednesday the congestion left, and I tested positive for COVID-19. Thursday I just felt a little tired and thought the worst was over. Friday, I woke up with vertigo that lasted for twelve hours and developed tinnitus. Saturday, I could not move from the fatigue. The severe fatigue lasted until the next Wednesday. I had no appetite the entire time. Then I lost all taste and smell. The fatigue continued. I am certain one of the children was the carrier. They were unscathed, thank God, with no symptoms and I believe I would have been in the hospital if I were not vaccinated. But there were weak emotional moments lying on the couch, barely able to move, that I, in the quietude of being alone and ill, even the mountains and the stream did not console me. But the idea of seeing the children again always snuggled me to comfort and sleep.

12-15-21

It has been four weeks since my confirmation with COVID-19. Most of the symptoms have left except for the severe fatigue, the tinnitus, and I still have not regained my sense of taste or smell. This has been an inconvenience, but it also can be dangerous, and I must be careful about what I eat and be more aware of what's going on in the house. I can't smell, for example burnt toast. I can't taste if something is sour or bad. But I have been able to maintain my Qigong morning workouts and I believe they have helped me chase off the virus and exponentially increase the healing. The extreme fatigue has tempered work on the house, but I have been able to accomplish a few things. The last few weeks have been pregnant with cold and rainy conditions, so my work in the stream has stalled.

12-23-21

I left the mountains traveling to Kentucky to see the children over Christmas. It is a short drive but beautiful through the Blue Ridge and Smoky mountains. Since I've moved here from the flatland of Georgia, the trip is much more palatable and beautiful driving through the high country and saves me approximately three hours on the trip each way. Christmas is just another day, if not for those two beautiful souls. So, I packed up the car with some extra presents that Santa dropped here and off I went. The mountains stayed with me for about two thirds of the trip as I drove through Tennessee, Virginia and across the state line into Kentucky ,and they did not vanish until I passed London, KY and picked up I71 North. Although the radio kept me company, its sound sank into the background along with the road noise and the stream of memories flowed freely accompanying me along the highway.

Christmas Eve and Christmas Day on 18th street with eleven people living in that small house was about as lucky as a small boy could ever be (I tend to rethink this now that it's fifty years later when considering Harry and Margaret Annie and their visits to the mountains). Santa came there on Christmas Eve night, because it was a way to help him out and cut down on some of his stress and his Christmas Day load. So, my uncle drove us around to see the Christmas lights adorning the houses in Louisville while Santa came to drop off the presents. This worked out well since the next day, Christmas Day, was the busiest day on 18th street. Relatives I had not seen except at first communion parties, confirmation parties or funerals all came to pay respects and to see Nannie, the matriarch of the family. As I played with my building blocks, Lincoln logs and Flintstone building blocks, and erector sets; a river of people flooded into the small house immediately after morning church services staying late into the day to see and pay homage to this wonderful patron saint of the city sidewalks, my great-grandmother, Nannie.

But being the inquisitive child I was, one Christmas I asked my grandfather, "We don't have a chimney in the house so how is Santa going to get in to deliver presents?" He was my surrogate father and, in my eyes, the kindest, most beautiful soul I have ever known.

He said, "Timmy," that is what he called me, "Timmy, we do have a fireplace so don't worry."

And as he said this he went to the attic and pulled out a box and took it downstairs to the small living room. He opened it and pulled out flat cardboard with a red brick pattern printed on the surface. Then he pulled out a piece of cardboard painted black. He bent and locked the pieces together and forming red cardboard pillars on each side of a small opening forming a hearth and locked them together with a black cardboard mantle. Then he placed a piece of cardboard shaped as flames, red, yellow, and orange in the hearth. Behind it was a tiny lightbulb and a stand. He plugged it in and then placed a small circular piece of aluminum balanced on top of the bulb that looked like a miniature ceiling fan. As the lightbulb heated, it rocked and spun the aluminum around producing a flickering light and shadows behind the cardboard flames. We had a fireplace on 18th Street for Santa.

While I was visiting the children at their home in Kentucky, the snow fell on Christmas Day morning, picturesque and solemn. I was on the first floor of the house before any creatures were stirring, doing Qigong and looking out the east window across the property at one of the oldest certified dogwood trees in North America appearing to float in the landscape with the falling snowflakes. An hour or so later, Harry woke and came downstairs, and glowed with the beauty of an innocent childhood. Margaret Annie came down soon after and as they were opening their presents deposited under the tree, I drifted looking out the window at the magnificent dogwood tree next to a brilliant holly tree while the snow lightly fell. No matter where I am, I am home when in the presence of the children. I have seen this scene repeated thirteen times and it only becomes more priceless every Christmas. After a few days there, sharing meals, stories, Nerf Gun battles, movies and assembling three Lego sets, it was time to return to the mountains. Leaving is always unbearable, but I know there are more glorious times to come.

The trip back offered the same beautiful scenery enhanced by the remnants of the snow that covered the tri-states, lingering in many areas through the mountains. The day was sunny and warm, but the frosting still hung tight to the north facing slopes, stubborn. When I crossed the Tennessee state line my anticipation grew to be home and feel the strength of my mountain again. I finally turned onto the gravel road as I have done one hundred times, never tiring of the climb, the gravel, the smell, the sound, and the energy. I stopped on the bridge, for a moment, to take in the sound of the water. I felt the stream welcoming me like an old dog on the front porch waiting for me to arrive. As I drove across the bridge, the stream seemed to let out a delicate sigh, a sigh of relief matching mine in harmony. Then once again, hearing the water, I am home.

Laurel Creek after a gentle winter snow.

Chapter XII

1-14-22

Snow fell overnight, heavy wet snow, blowing stinging sideways snow, forcing the rhododendrons to bow, looking like a Georgia cotton field holding the small white puffs atop of their evergreen leaves and layering a row of white frosting on every horizontal branch covered in tenuous balance. Snow blanketed the mountains, the gravel road, the open flatter areas west to Watauga Lake, Mount Gilead, Roan Mountain, Banner Elk, Seven Devils, Valle Crucis and east through the city streets of Boone and Blowing Rock. According to all who have lived here for more than forty years, it was snow reminiscent of "the normal snow;" common snow, staying-for-weeks-snow which capped these mountains fifteen years ago, but which has slowly vanished and has become scarce. It hugged the top of every power line along the highways sagging the lines, increasing the bottom black inverted arch between poles. It covered every mountain switchback, every rooftop, every vehicle left in the open, every piece of exposed farm equipment, every fence post holding cattle and horses, and every road sign and every small bridge. The snow was held by every tree, but prominently by the pines at the upper elevations testing the bows of these giants, and sometimes punishing them. The snow not caught by the trees made its way to the streams and rivers like countless beautiful floating white paratroopers assaulting the tributaries silently, slowly, deliberately, and secretly raising the water level. Unlike the rain, we are often fooled by the snow's beauty, and we are numb to the weight as it accumulates and sneaks upon us as thieves in the night.

Then, in the darkness, combined with the whistling sound of mountain wind I heard a slow "craaaccckkkk," then a louder quicker crack, then a long violent crash behind the house echoing up the mountain. In the morning I looked out the rear north side window up the mountain and saw a twelve-inch diameter walnut tree lodged between an oak and a pine that had given way from the snow and wind, uprooted, and resting on these other two pillars. A casualty of war between the soil and wind and the snow. But the loss will yield firewood, forest mulch, and open the woods to new sunlight. It is an unpredictable and constantly repeated energy exchange in nature.

The snow covered the bridge, thirteen inches thick, easily measured. It covered the upper rail, rounded mounds continuously across the length mating with the gravel road. It covered the wood base planks hidden beneath the white seen as a contrast from the side. There I compared the thickness of the bridge planks that are four inches thick to their covering now thirteen inches. As the state ploughed the gravel road, they threw mounded snow up across my drive at the bridge to a depth of two feet. Suddenly I received a call from Liz telling me Tom had his tractor rigged with snow chains and he had just finished their drive and was on his way to plough my bridge before he put the machine away.

Tom came to the rescue like a superhero apparition perched on his tractor rolling down the snow-covered gravel road with a front-end loader attachment, dressed in his insulated coveralls, hooded jacket, with an invisible "S" on his chest and plowed the bridge as it began to snow lightly again. Although he loves to get on his tractor for any reason, this was the epitome of mountain neighboring and shows the kindness he possesses. When he arrived, I met him at the bottom of the drive.

"It's about time you got out and did some work," I said jokingly.

"Well, I just figured I'd get some air on this beautiful day," he replied.

"I was speaking to the neighbors, and we were wondering when you were going to clean your yard up, it's looking a little ratty," I said facetiously knowing his yard and house were always kept disgustingly perfect.

"Well, I guess since I missed the last meeting of the HOA, they are kicking me out. I was never a good member anyway," he laughed.

There is no HOA in the mountains, and I smiled, and said, "Thank you, you're a good man and are very kind to help me."

Within an hour he had the entire bridge cleaned and cleared. He too, told me this was a regular occurrence up to fifteen years ago and it happened at least a dozen times during those winters in days of yore. "But not lately," he said then drove away across the bridge, right on the snow-covered gravel road and home to be warmed next to his wood burning stove. The next day I delivered bread I'd made and a gift certificate for dinner at the local restaurant, a slight show of appreciation for his kindness.

The outline of the stream is dark flowing and vivid seen through the kitchen window. The air temperature makes it too cold for me to work in the stream and the snow has stopped the work on the steps. In just one day the sunshine was vanquished by darkened skies, the temperature dropped from the mid-forties, and snow covered the area. Yesterday I was able to work the stream briefly. I have a small fire going in the wood stove, damper open, slight air feeding the fire and it is keeping the house at sixty-five degrees with outside temperature of twenty-six. The teapot atop the wood stove serenades me with a light slight whistle as the water stays hot forcing the steam through the spout. The snow is unbreeched currently and is pure and perfect bordering the stream sides. Rocks heated by yesterday's sun have refused to allow the snow to cover them and set proudly apart while the soil and other shaded rocks are covered in white. As I was standing at the sink drinking my tea made from water that I boiled on the wood stove top, I spotted a blur of movement in the stream. I fetched my binoculars and spotted the blue heron walking the middle of the stream one deliberate shifting slow step at a time.

Step, step, step, then a pause, then a cock of her head, a stretch of her neck, looking upstream, bobbing, and shifting adjusting her view, then another step then a pause then two steps and a pause. She seemed oblivious to the air temperature, water temperature and wind whipping across the mountains funneling along the stream focusing on her mission. Her head remained still and fixed in space as her body moved first, followed by her neck, then the last to move was her head. I had just worked on the stream yesterday for a few hours before the temperature and snow began to drop, moving rocks from the center and this offered her new hunting grounds. Her tiny thin legs barely broke a wake in the icy water. She continued her stalking upstream fifty yards repeating the same stealthy march.

I can only assume she is there because she knows there is a food source, an affirmation of a healthy stream, but maybe she is just liking the scenery and is taking a stroll through the frigid water on this beautiful day when all else had slowed due to the snow. Suddenly she decided her walk needed to end. She stopped, bent her thin nimble legs, moved her wings above her head bent at the midpoint, leapt into the air while spreading her wings up then down in one powerful stroke of five feet wide feather and muscle and was airborne. It is obvious where the Qigong masters invented and mimicked this movement, they call the crane, demonstrated in nature here by this graceful bird. Several more flaps of the huge wings sent her gliding down just four feet above the water and precisely inside the tree canopy like a skilled fighter pilot. Then for a reason only she knows, and a place only she has chosen, she accelerated and rose above and out of the stream area and tree canopy.

She is the magical icon of flight hovering above the stream on the breadth of the mountains. She appears to know no season, unlike our summer friend Jimmy, the water snake, who is an animal of the warmer seasons, cold blooded, and who is bound to the earth. But both these creatures have overlapping existences found in the bosom of the water and the stream. Both draw life from the veins of the water and connect with its energy. But make no mistake, given the opportunity the predator could be the prey. The Heron will hunt the water snake with no mercy if the opportunity presents itself. The symbolism is extraordinary. An air creature drawing life from the earth creature via the water in order that she may leave the earth to take flight from nourishment. Again, the connectivity of the stream is simple and brilliant.

Papa's Old Coat
Pencil on Paper
Mark T. Wright

Mine was the first steps, to violate the pristine surface, first to help Tom plow the bridge and lower parking area, then to walk the stream edge basking in this glorious white light of the snow and stream. No deer tracks, no mink tracks, no crow or blue jay, no cardinals, no muskrat, no titmouse, no other footprints graced this area until mine. No other life showed along the stream until the next morning when gorgeous sunlight began to melt the snow mounds and a single meandering line of multiple deer tracks dashed the snow plane in perfect order. The water flowed as it did the day before, but something is different other than the starkly defined edges of water against the pure white powder. Few cars traveled the gravel road to interrupt the music of the stream while every chimney billowed smoke in winter unison, easier to see against the white background.

The snow stopped and the sun emerged blindingly bright, reflecting off the white mirror. Despite the bridge being clear the gravel road was not safely passable unless with a four-wheel drive or snow chains attached to your wheels. I was snowed in but at peace with the idea, knowing it was temporary; and it gave me permission to reflect and think and walk carefully shin deep in snow along the stream, knowing that the mountains will soon be giving the snow back to the stream swelling it gradually. Peace in this place gave way to a heightened spirituality as nature humbled me and befriended me with its dangerous beauty.

1-20-22

The temperature has risen above freezing, and in combination with the sunshine the snow has left, relegated to saturating the soil as liquid water migrating through the land into the stream. The metal roof of the house growls at me as it heats up and the snow moves and slides down across its surface ending with small crashes on the deck. Soon the entire red roof became exposed as the snow melted. As the temperature rose so did the stream level, silently and deliberately and deceptively without fanfare or credit from the clouds. The south facing mountain sides were the first to lose the blanket, initially at the upper levels then migrating and eroding minute by minute down across the level fields. The highest level of the mountain where the pines dwell is still the coldest, and the snow held by these soldiers stays white and steadfast and is a content prisoner of these benevolent captors. As the temperature rises, a darker partially green band appears in the mountains between the pines and lower-level birches, where the snow, exposed to the direct sun, has melted back to the land. After several days of the higher temperatures the band migrated across the lower levels, across the stream, but stops on the north facing mountain slopes devoid of direct sunlight. Here, sometimes for days, and even with temperatures in the fifties, the snow is stubborn to leave encouraged by those north slopes. There small snowy patches dot the darker hillsides and from a distance tease us with melting images of the springtime and mirages of white milkweed.

2-20-22

As a side effect of the COVID-19 virus I have lost my sense of smell and taste, have tinnitus, and I have isolated pain in my forearms that will not leave as well as relentless fatigue. It was fortuitous that in December and January this year the mountains often became blanketed with light snow and lower temperatures. Beautiful as winter is in the mountains, the work stopped on the stream. So, I worked on the inside of the house, cleaning, caulking, insulating, and painting.

2-22-22

The weather finally broke, and I have been able to move into the stream on more occasions to work small sections on select days when the temperature rose above 40 degrees. I witness a beautiful momentum of positive energy occurring as the stream reacts to the changes and the restoration. The snow melted and the rain came, and the path of water followed and moved as we planned. The stream overflowed its banks as it should in controlled areas, and then the water flow reduced, and the stream maintained the new structure. Maybe nature is placating me with this tease of success and an attempt to boost my spirits after the COVID-19 experience. Regardless, I'll take it.

The stream keeps helping me deepen the center channel naturally in concert with the new consistent and accelerated water flow and bedrock. The rocks that I placed have modified the current to create multiple wonderful areas for fish. Other areas have gathered sediment showing me where I must do more work. The balance between water flow and sediment transfer, water velocity and action, meandering movement and erosion control is a fluid dance controlled by the stream and water. They can be coaxed but not ruled, can be lead and modified but not challenged. This is the work for me as a steward and as a partner. Each rock modifies the actions, the butterfly effect again in its perfect explanation.

She teaches me, exposing the work that is futile, and when the work is insightful and then elevates the profundity to brilliance before my eyes, or removes it with the next rain, and over time. I tend to work upstream first and then move downstream. I sometimes skip around in small hundred-foot sections upstream, downstream, and side to side because my action in one place changes the action elsewhere. I sometimes can predict the effects with reserved certainty and confidence, but other times they are glorious discoveries in this partnership. Then those discoveries initiate other solutions and still other wonderful discoveries.

Another hard rain occurred, and the stream's water volume and velocity increased, becoming more brilliant as it washes sediment and years of neglect downstream. Every change and improvement I make, I pray for rain to engorge the stream washing through my work and cleansing away the dirt exposing the natural beauty. Each time this happens I feel as if the grit removed from my soul is washed downstream. The more I work, the more I comprehend this conversation with the stream and the water, and the easier it becomes to only do what I believe is acceptable by the stream. The goal is to do the least amount of work and cause the least amount of intrusion to the stream to achieve the maximum effect toward balance. Initial movements are a prelude to the final modifications since this is a living entity and if you do not understand the process, you might think it was a waste of time.

But it is not. I learned, was taught, that often there must be preparation, then a test, then a retest and a test when the flood comes, and a test when it is a drought, and a test when it is normal, and a test when it rains, and test when a rock is moved, and a test when a channel is dug and a test when a deeper hole is developed, and a test when an undercut bank is reinforced, and a test when there are diverters placed, and a test when the bank is sloped, and a test when the stream is made meandering, and a test when the channel is deepened, and a test when silt is removed, and a test when the larger rocks are removed from the bottom, and a test when rocks are added as displacement and when rocks are added barriers, and a test when rocks are impediments to slow the flow and test of patience and resolve. The first steps are simple, but a daunting task. Refinement is revelation.

2-27-22

It has been raining for six days straight which is beneficial for the rivers and streams to wash away the silt and expose the gravel bottoms. Mid-week the rain pummeled the area, adding more water and the stream overflowed its banks in a daunting but predictable rush. The main structures seem adequate to maintain the stream form. The water is helping me deepen areas and transport silt after I have narrowed the stream width and increased the water velocity. I am attempting to maintain relative stream balance when there is normal flow, which allows the channel to overflow in a controlled way when it floods.

In March, the state will stock fish above and below this eight-hundred feet section of stream moving through my property. I believe some fish will migrate up and down the stream and I will try to make sure no one trespasses and takes out the fish from my property. I will have to police it strongly, so people do not take out fish and kill them. I have posted signs along the property. Now we will have to be vigilant and police this to make sure violators stay away.

The children came down last week and Harry rushed to the stream immediately. I had been removing the sand from part of the stream and depositing it on the bank so he could build sandcastles and forts. He loves the sand and digging and any opportunity to build his castles. It is such a joy to see him make this his own and play so innocently. It is a gift to be with him and help him build the castles. I would drift stick boats down and by his castles and he would bomb them with rocks as they drift by. We did this for hours. Then the action moved to dropping rocks off the bridge and watching them explode into the flooding waters below. The atomic splash was so intense it reached Harry on top of the bridge.

Harry dug and pulled and searched for rocks as big as his head and as big as he could carry to haul them up the banks to the bridge. Then Margaret Annie joined in the play. He struggled to climb the bank carrying the missile, the steep slope did not deter him, and it was worth it in the end. They then lifted the bombs over the bridge rail, and I would give the countdown, three…two…one…go, and they dropped the rocks and watched them hit the water in a double mushroom splash and he screamed with giddy excitement and pure innocent joy, "Whoa!" He would only stop when he asked me, "Papa, my hands are cold. Can we go up?" He refused to wear gloves even though I insisted and knew where it was going, I let him go on as long as he wanted.

When we were out at the stream, we had conversations about his castles and his motes and his strategy to protect his fort. He overheard on the news about the invasion of Ukraine by Russia, and he wanted to know what that meant. So, I told him there are sometimes evil people in the world who try to hurt other people. And what we need to do is say prayers for the Ukrainian people, the children. I told him that the people of Russia do not want this, but one man; the president, is evil and runs the country by force, fear, and hurts anyone who objects to what he does. The people of Ukraine want to be free and left alone but the Russian president is the one who wants to hurt them. Harry loves tanks and we watched the *Age of Tanks* show and remembered the Russian tanks shown in a later episode reflecting the year 1980. I showed him pictures of the current Russian tanks and he thought they were the same tanks, and then after his lengthy comparisons of the details it appeared he was correct in his observation. I know he understood the tragedy at a basic level because Margaret Annie asked about the war and Harry gave a clear and concise explanation.

Harry surveying the steam and spotting fish.

Later, on the world map, I showed Harry where his house was in Kentucky compared to North Carolina, where we are and where Russia is, and where Ukraine is. I explained we have so many connections and that the same water in the stream, makes its way to the Watauga River, then onto the Holston River, moving onto the Tennessee river, to the confluence with the Ohio river, then onto the Mississippi river and then onto the Gulf of Mexico. The water in the ocean and air could be the same water the Ukrainian and Russian people touch and could make its way back to us here in the natural cycle. I explained that there are free countries around Russia that are frightened and wary because they feared they could be next, and Putin might not stop with Ukraine. Harry understood this and told Margaret Annie about it. His little mind understood good and evil in context, the need to pray for the children, and he understood about a bully and how Putin is hurting innocent people. It is so amazing that he and Margaret Annie understood and have compassion for the children and understood the concept of the bully. Then we went onto playing a *Star Wars* video game and making bread and hot cocoa to warm chilled bodies. The beauty of a child.

A blue heron visits every day. Yesterday she stood on a large rock in the middle of the stream. She was motionless for several minutes slowly moving her neck straight out at a thirty-degree angle parallel to the waterflow, stretched to her maximum. Then slowly her neck became drawn back and formed a graceful meandering shape like a snake. Her head tilted to the left, and she seemed to gaze down at the water directly adjacent to the rock. Then suddenly she struck down with almost unperceivable speed. The water parted with a huge splash, and she speared something in the water below. Her head came up and kicked back as she tossed the prize slightly repositioning it so it would slide into her mouth and down her throat. She waited there for a moment and flew off. Her presence assured me there was life in the stream that she fancied.

The stream is giving me more than I expected but all that I hoped for. And it speaks to Harry drawing him like a beacon as soon as he arrives. That simple power, that simple rush and energy, that wonderful life has shown itself to me and my children. The challenging work has been more than worth it both physically and emotionally. The sometimes visceral sometimes extremely calculated action of moving rocks and clearing a path for the water, sometimes is clean and simple, other times it is a wonderful folly celebrated between me and the stream. People only see the results of the design and effort but do not see the work, the continuous adjustments of the new water, the success, the failures. But we can only achieve enlightenment by doing. The stream life is flourishing where it did not before I started. Turning over rocks expose colonies of mayflies and stonefly nymphs, crayfish and small salamanders, small minnows and tadpoles, and water spiders galore already. And it is only the edge of spring. Soon the plant life will begin to emerge and add another dimension to the stream banks bringing more life and providing areas for the water insects to emerge and take cover. I have nothing but humbling smiles. There is more work to do.

3-10-22

In the beginning of Spring, I planted forsythia along the lower side bank hoping they will migrate along the edge helping to restore the riparian area. The plants should aid in stabilizing the banks, add more cover to the stream to cool it, and provide cover for the stream life. I also relocated burning bushes around a drainage outlet and up a small slope. I plan to place evergreen plants such as azaleas, rhododendrons, and holly trees above the riparian area to add cover year-round and stabilize the bank structure. I started with small pine saplings, but the deer decided they were tasty and ate all thirteen plants. I will try again in the fall.

3-13-22

Surprise frigid temperatures and snow crept across the mountains silently through the night. At first light there is no break in the brilliant purity of the snow, no steps no prints, and no disruption in the brilliant blanket, except for the stream that looks like a thick huge peaceful charcoal drawing line against the brilliant snow landscape interrupted by the darker walnut trees. The edge of the bank shows off brilliantly and perfectly when the snow comes, and the stream does not freeze. The water moves slowly kissing the bank and the rocks, standing as a stone gauntlet captures the snow and makes simple meandering edges not as apparent without the snow. It is a moving flowing charcoal drawing, pairing the meandering stream against the straight and strong road above it outlined against the snow. The width of the streamline is dark and continuous with specs of boulders peeking above the water line dusted with snow, touched with water moving and frozen. Most of the stream is clearly showing, with some areas pinched solid and frozen along the bank edges providing a glazed transition between snow and water. The ice sneaks from the snow creeping slowly across the water's edges attempting to choke the stream width and steal the surface water converting it to a solid. However, the stream partners with the water and resists the freezing temperatures with its gallant movement, and so far has yielded cautiously and quietly but continues moving slowly downstream. The water in the stream has taken on a new fluid stubbornness and appears proud as it continues to flow and fight against the below freezing temperatures; its unseen mysterious adversary pushing it to stillness. The jousting between temperature and the partners of the water and the stream is an amazing phenomenon to watch. We always pray the prized scarf stays with the water.

3-27-22

The daytime temperatures rose to the normal mid-forties and I was in the stream again. The first spring stocking by the state has just happened in streams and rivers in the area. Al was back from Charlotte and came by to check on progress, say hello and politely exaggerate about his fishing escapades. And I mean exaggerate in a wonderful, humorous angler type of way. I was adjusting the stones at the falls near the bridge to shift the water flow in a continuous "S" pattern directing it away from the pier. I wanted the falls to step and create slower areas where a fish could rest to make it upstream but still have enough water flow to oxygenate the stream water below. Al parked near the mailboxes alongside the road and walked over to where I was working. It was a few minutes after two.

"Hey Mark, just got done and had a great day out there today...ended up catching a dozen fish in a small stream up the road. I was euro nymphing and they tore it up! Caught one real nice rainbow…fifteen inches on a white and black nymph with a red-hot spot. I let it drift in the current then back drift in the reverse eddies and it hit like a ton."

"Yes, he was facing the other direction from the main current but facing against the eddies current…fantastic! Wow, that was a good day my friend." I spoke.

"I'm amazed that you're doing the work yourself and can do it at our age," Al said.

I told him, "Al, I feel so fortunate to be able to shape this stream to be vibrant again.

He asked, "have you seen any more fish."

I replied, "A few, and one nice rainbow cruising downstream like he owned the place oblivious to me; and all kinds of other life that supports the fish like salamanders, nymphs, crawdads, sculpins, and a huge number of minnows. I hope more come back when the weather warms a bit more."

"Well, I need to go. My wife is waiting, and I need to finish cutting up that tree that fell a while back before we head home to Charlotte. I'm back next month so let's get together and I'll show you those spots."

"It's a deal my friend, be safe going back and thanks for stopping."

I had to share details of my trip with the children and their tremendous success as anglers. As I worked, we talked about barometric pressure, line weights, moon phases and water flow. All these things are basic vocabulary of anglers. We talked of trout, bluegill, bass and shoal bass and our experiences. He asked me about bass fishing. This was a type of fishing that I cut my teeth on in Kentucky and Georgia, but I fancy the stream fishing for trout now. There is something universal about angling and the common bond of the joy of fishing.

Laurel Creek Late Autumn
Pencil on paper
Mark T. Wright

4/7/22

There came an intense rain last night that kept me awake, pummeling the metal roof like I have not heard since I have lived here. The next morning, the water did not flood the banks violently. It followed the center channel for a while, then overflowed more deliberately controlled in an uncontrollable route and where it discharged more energy. It then receded more quickly back into the center channel. The new narrowed meandering route helps increase the water velocity washing silt away while also helping dissipate the floods energy. The stones added at the banks further buffer and help subdue the water's destructive erosion. The birch trees seemed content cradled by the reinforced arms of the stones at the bank. So far it is working but nature has its moments to humble us and keep us sober. I celebrate with restricted optimism.

I have been working on the stream for five days between gaps in the rain. I have been deepening runs and placing stones at the bank to help stop the erosion. I have noticed that sculpins have come back and are darting around as I disturb their hiding places. I am anxious to see if any more trout return or have hatched in the stream. The labor is more difficult as the water gets deeper. I make huge efforts before each rain anticipating that the rain will assist me in the work.

4-13-22

There has been no rain for days, I am able to work and adjust the depths accordingly. When it comes, the rain increases the water volume in the stream, and now concentrates the water to the restored center channel and not toward the bank's edges eroding the soil. The increased flow of water washes more sediment away and exposes the rock and gravel bottoms.

By reducing the erosion and refining the water flow, decreasing sediment here, decreases the impact of the sediment downstream. The sediment occurring from land run off and erosion will continue until I can shore up the banks (no pun intended) and promote new vegetation in the riparian areas. Placing stones at the bank as well as planting more trees and vegetation restore the riparian zone helping to keep hold of the soil at the same time filtering the runoff and sediment.

As I work in the center channel, I realize by relocating any rock and boulder over eight inches in diameter, I will promote the current to quickly deepen the channel. This is a beautiful event, and the initial wash of stone happens quickly. The current exorcises the sediment and exposes new rock faces and new environments for insects, crustaceans, salamanders and fish. Over time this process continues and strikes an equilibrium of current to rock face that reveals a layered random stack of rock edge stepping from the bottom of the stream bedrock up. It is a miniature landscape of underwater cliffs and caverns brilliant and beautiful.

4-18-22

I have been assessing the methods that I have used to get the stream to this stage. The successful solution for the small stream seems to be redirecting the energy of the stream by changing the direction of flow back and forth in a meandering form and creating a center channel narrow enough to sustain water flow year-round. This has been a slow direct process helping the stream rehabilitate with crutches of structures, later reducing them to canes, and then the stream absorbing them into the family and moving on its own. None of these structures I built exist in their pristine original form. Each structure, continually shaped by the water and stream, morphs into a natural mutated magical form. Since I do not have an overabundance of land and am working within the confines of the stream banks, I had to invent ways to redirect the flow with depth and diverter rocks to train the stream to move in the meandering pattern, while at the same time narrowing the stream width due to the finite amount of water flowing in the stream

5-3-22

I worked eight hours in the stream today. The work concentrated on deepening the center section of the channel and eliminating the areas of silt build up. Additionally, I worked on deepening areas beside and on the downstream side of large boulders to make haven for small animals. It has not rained in days and the weather predicted storms, so I stopped on the steps and focused back on the stream before the rain came.

I saw more sculpins, several small rainbows and the first small water snake today while working. There are minnows and crayfish and an enormous number of nymphs and salamanders. I stood motionless and watched the route the rainbow took downstream. It followed a haphazard route, but I am sure it was logical in the mind of the trout. It was wonderful to watch the fish move slowly then scurry then wait then move again darting in and out of boulders swimming with the current. It took the slowest current route, even swimming downstream. Or it was taking the route with the most shadows since fish have no eyelids. Or took the most scenic route along that portion of the stream. The reason is irrelevant. The important thing was that it was a route and that it was beautiful.

Seeing the rainbow trout was a gift and a surprise for me. A gift I interpreted as the stream becoming acceptable to hold fish again. To my overwhelming joy, it appears the work is helping the stream environment become conducive to supporting life at multiple levels and that what I am doing is not in vain. This was a friend passing by on a grand adventure. It was moving quietly in safe waters. It showed me that prehistoric instinct and senses we can only wonder of were guiding this small animal through the underwater maze and that what I was doing to restore the stream to balance might be acceptable and recognizable to the small life.

I went back downstream to see if any fish had taken up residence in the new water. I took my flyrod to evaluate the flow of the water, the obstacles and to see if I might hook a small fish. I started with a small nymph at the bridge and after thirty casts hooked a small rainbow. I then fished spots working my way upstream with small hits by small fish. I changed to a dry fly pattern, a small green drake. I had made my way to the end of the upper section using extreme stealth. I cast the fly and let it drift without luck. I then cast it to an impossible spot, a small beautiful six-inch brook trout took the fly.

As I slowly brought this beautiful little creature closer, I broke a tear of gratitude that this small animal graced me with this moment. Graced me with the affirmation that I may be doing something correctly with the stream and the water. Graced me with its presence and its showing of its magnificent colors. Graced me with the knowledge of the disconnected moments of my life and work are in fact intimately connected and have allowed another brilliant moment to intervene in the timeline. As I asked it to calm down so we could part expeditiously, it heard me. I wet my hand in the stream and cupped the small fish gently as I removed the barbless hook fly from its mouth. As I reached down and placed it back into the water I said, "Thank you, thank you for this and stay healthy here." It lingered for a moment just below the water surface and then moved away quickly back into the main stream, disappearing, and blending into its environment; its soul contract fulfilled for that moment as it shared a spiritual connection with me. We were supposed to meet, touch, and go on. And for a startling minute as I floated above the stone and water, I experienced the same magic I had over and over and over for forty years, and I drew strength from this experience unlike a captive Antaeus who lost strength as his feet left the earth.

Kentucky Crusher Streamers. Flies I hand tied.

5-10-22

Traci stopped by in her four-wheeled drive jeep and dropped off a potted plant and told me, "Congratulations, you've been living in the house for one year!"

I was amazed. It felt like it could be one month or twenty years. I reflected on all I had accomplished and all I had not accomplished, what solutions worked and what failed to work. I could tell she was slightly surprised at the work completed and she did not realize the amount of work remaining. I said, "Traci, I knew but did not want you to make an issue of it for Wayne's sake. That's what I do and I'm so fortunate I know how and can still do the work."

"Have you spoken to Wayne at all? I just loved this sister, but his squeeze out in New Mexico is crazy," she said.

"Yes, I went to see him last month; he's living in the old Cove Stream mill. A great place but an insane amount of work and he is having trouble seeing and getting around. I think he's trying to get his son to help but I didn't know. How are the kids?"

We spoke awhile longer about our kids, the weather, how her work was going, and she was off quickly to her next appointment and her next closing.

The pain in my arms and hands, the browning of the lower part of my arms from the sun; my waders that are finally leaking from the abuse; the eleven pairs of gloves that have been worn to shreds; and one wooden shovel handle snapped in two, are all benchmarks in the process and a year worth of effort. I cannot stop striving for improvement. The physical and emotional struggle, fortified in the stream, has become an irrevocable spiritual journey exposing what makes us truly human. Anything less denies our full humanity.

It finally rained tonight at a steady pace for a short while. I am always anxious to see how it affects the stream. It seems like little rain in total, but I hope the runoff will be much greater and stream swells carrying silt away and deepening the channel that I outlined. It is ironic to me, when I ran the construction projects, weather, rain, cold and snow were always on my mind because inclement weather impeded work, stopped the schedules, and lost money. Now I welcome moderate rain like a stream farmer to invigorate the stream but worry about the extremes as I did years ago.

There was a light half inch rain the last few days. I worked in the stream yesterday for seven hours specifically on a twenty-five-yard section on the upper side. I have divided the upper quarter of the stream into sections to control work efforts. The upper section begins with a rapid section of falls just off my property. This feeds into a wider section, beginning my property of slower flat water with deep runs. Then there is a small diverter with a slight drop to another wider slower section of water. It moves then to a more severe drop that I have stair stepped and made rapids, but they are still fish negotiable. The next section just below the rapids is another small deeper area but still more narrow to achieve a slightly faster water flow before changing the elevation again to a slight drop. Each section is a test. Each area has completely different water flow at the surface and below at different depths, has different cover, different shape, different rock, and boulder formations. Each area is diverse and a working Petri dish and a test to explore what life responds to each section. The problem is I only know what I can see, and the magic hopefully happens beyond my eyes.

5-23-22

I worked yesterday in a five-star hotel of a brook trout stream. I walked the stream up and down studying the small section on my property but also, I walked another quarter mile downstream fishing and studying the details of the natural stream. I observed the difficulties, the good and bad where I saw fish and where I caught fish. Then I went back to my area of the stream to mend holes and refine the work, taking inspiration from the best untouched natural sections of the stream.

It rained hard for the first time in weeks and as a result the wash and run off limestone dust from the gravel road turned the stream to a milky white/grey flowing line. It was an x-ray of the image of the stream in the winter when it snowed and created a reverse visual. Here and now the water was milky grey and the edges clear and sharp against the flora. In winter against the snow, it was a clear black flowing pencil line, exposing in exactitude the edges of the stream and every protruding boulder peeking above the surface level of the water.

I worked on the downstream section of the stream, and I observed where I needed to deepen and carve out more stream to allow water to flow more freely. The water temperature was already at a little less than sixty-five degrees, borderline for trout. I will monitor the temperature carefully and hope it stays or drops in temperature. Any higher and the fish are stressed. But having the water temperature at sixty-five degrees in June with elevated air temperatures and limited rain is a wonderful surprise.

I work continuously and as often as possible to prepare for the fall when working days decrease, and the temperatures drop, and the rain comes. The work to make the stream continually communicate after breaking the dams, has been a monumental task. But as with building accessible ramps to building entrances ,the lowest possible slope to get up in elevation is parallel to the grade. This is not the shortest distance from "point a to point b," but it is the gentlest slope. So, to help flatten out the severe drops that have developed, I have built diverter ramps perpendicular to the stream flow to gradually allow the water to flow and communicate to the lower areas. The meandering stream will assist this also, but concentrated quicker drops are necessary in some areas.

These water ramps will accelerate the water flow and allow fish to communicate back and forth up stream. It is a hook and a water ramp with a retaining wall on the downstream force side, redirecting water from in line flow to perpendicular flow to the main flow of the stream. This redirects the water, changes direction, oxygenates the water, varies the current, and instead of a waterfall it is a constant flow of water connecting the sections. Where before there was a waterfall that was difficult to navigate or nonnegotiable by the trout, there is now a water connection in its place.

6-9-22

The temperature is hotter than normal, and I was working on a small section of the stream to deepen the bed directly after a waterfall. However, the water still flows around my legs cooling me even in this warmer temperature. Still, I feel exhausted today by the heat, but I am going back to work in that area. Today I will take the temperature and depth measurement throughout the stream, hoping that the stream will maintain temperatures below sixty-eight degrees, even in the dead of summer period.

I worked in the middle section after developing a deep pool at a small cross vein that focused water to the center. The stream is incredibly low. Rainfall for this period is below average but if I can make the stream work at the lowest water level life will flourish when there is normal rainfall. As in all partnerships, it is easy when there are robust times, but the real test comes when the waters are low.

I have chosen to keep and work around existing boulders that appear to have been in the stream for centuries, wrought with clues on the path that the stream wants to take. Presently, they stick their heads above the water causing white bubbling foam at the surface around their bodies, and still pocket water below the surface on their downstream side. Submerged during normal water levels, these stones still cause varied underwater currents. But daily, in summer dry months there is less and less water flowing, and I am shooting at a moving target as I try to keep water moving and water temperature down. Currently, the water is so low and problematic that in the morning I'll begin to work in an area to develop the proper flow and depth and by the evening the water level has dropped and inch or so and affecting the work. I am continually chasing the depleting water level like a dragon chasing his tail. The lower water level is conducive to working the stream bed, constructing the diverter, and cross veins, but it is a crapshoot and an educated guess as to the results when the rain does come, and the water level rises. Ideally it will improve the stream when this happens, and if the preparation is brilliant and perfect, then the stream will accept it fully. This is never the case and nature always humbles me with its surprises. I simply count on some success along with the many partial failures and relish the conversation that continues and the beauty that evolves.

I have had modest success in the middle section and upper sections of the stream developing the center channel. Depth, water flow, boulder placement, deep sections, all seemed to work swimmingly in unison and life is occupying this area. The water temperature is low, in the mid-sixties, the water is clear, shade and cover are abundant, oxygenation in this area is rich and riparian areas are reestablishing. Variations in current and structure are working in these areas fed by a long waterfall that opens to a wider section slowing the current but still allowing water to flow steadily transferring sediment.

Rainbow Trout I caught in Laurel Creek.

As I worked on the middle section of the stream just above the middle falls, a small six-inch trout rushed through and over the falls downstream. Then when I went below the falls to work, I spooked him again, and he scurried and darted back up the cascading falls, which now has an area that communicates freely upstream to its original spot. This was an amazing act to witness. This tiny torpedo shaped body, perfectly built to face upstream and hold in fast current now showed the agility and ability to swim upstream against gravity and current seeking the holding spot above the falls and where it began.

6-12-22

I was working in the middle and lower sections and observed small four to six inches fish moving about twelve to eighteen inches of water. It was refreshing that they were holding where they should be and where I had built and developed the interim sanctuaries along the stream route. I try to think as small fish would and attempt to build and work areas that will provide a sense of shelter, hiding and reduced current so they can rest and wait for the food to drift through. I sat and studied the smaller minnows in schools facing the current, they jockeyed for position with one another to be first in the food line. They sometimes appear to be playful and other times territorial nipping at each other, pushing and shoving one another around. Other times they all move in a beautiful syncopated underwater dance effectively choreographed and always facing upstream. They hold effortlessly in the current drifting backwards, slightly exchanging positions like a drafting cyclist then continue shifting their bodies constantly using dorsal, pectoral, and caudal fins elegantly adjusting positions. If these small animals can hold their positions, then larger fish can also.

Jimmy the small water snake was out investigating my raising a ruckus in the water and overturning rocks where his small prey may hide. I watched him gracefully slither under the water, hunting as the small minnows scattered in his presence. He moved slowly then stopped shifting just enough to stay stable in the current then placed himself beside a boulder in pocket water, and he expended the minimal amount of energy required to hold his position. Still, under the water searching. Then a short raise of his head above the surface to get a breath and then back under to the next rock and watching and waiting. On the next visit with the children, Margaret Annie promised me she could catch Bobby, the larger snake, and we would try to relocate him downstream. He is one of the apex predators along with the heron and the mink that will feast on the small fish. I will also continue to deepen areas and provide additional cover to help these fish, making the hunt more difficult for the predators.

This last week the air temperature was in the high eighties and the nighttime temperature did not reduce. So, work in the stream was laborious and arduous at best, even with my feet in cooling water. The work these last few days have been enjoyable, with life exploding all around me. The months of July and August promise to have the same higher temps. Rainfall is well below normal, but the prediction is it will accelerate in August. This has been the pattern here in the mountains as the hurricane season normally begins in August and lasts through November as the storms pass through the Gulf of Mexico and move moist air up and across the northeast, affecting the high country.

The rain has come in bursts of downpours with extended periods of dryness in between. The last storm dropped one inch of rain in a twelve-hour period in this portion of the mountains. One inch of rain barely makes an impact on the water when we experience extended dry periods, since the stream absorbs it quickly. The water will rise to a wonderful level then abruptly and sadly recede expeditiously since the ground is absorbing every drop, reducing runoff, and the elevated temperature encourages rapid evaporation. In this scenario less water makes it to the stream and although we think there was a hard rain, and it was, there is little direct impact on the stream.

Even with rain of one plus inches in a twelve-hour period, the rise in the stream is swift and the reduction the same. Due to the long delay between rain, each period washes the summer's limestone dust into the stream making it the milky grey color or the muddy brown color for the first hours. Quickly it subsides, and the clear mountain water resumes, and the stream takes on its magnificent lively attributes and diversity. Then as quickly as it came, nature snatches that titillating moment and establishes a compromised median that sustains the life, and we breathe a bit as it calms to a normal resting place. I watched as it slowly reduces and teeters on the brink of extinction as it waits for the life-giving rain again and the cycle restarts. I am lucky I am on the lower section of the stream before the confluence with the Watauga River, so I receive run off from all the rain upstream for miles. In the same breadth, I can be the recipient of a torrent due to the runoff upstream. I try to plan for this double-edged sword and hope I receive a nod from the bank and the birch trees that I have helped keep their place in this dance.

Margaret Annie in a quiet moment.

Chapter XIII

6-18-22

The children came down for a week to celebrate Father's Day. We fished, we hiked the waterfall, we hiked Grandfather Mountain, we hiked up the back mountain bushwacking and climbing like mountain goats. Harry made me a Father's Day card that was the best, depicting where I was in the ring with Iron Mike Tyson for the match for the #1 dad mug. Iron Mike was defeated by Papa after "eight minutes of "sparadik" punching." Margaret Annie's gift was a handmade spectacularly translucent colored sculpture that I have sitting in the kitchen window. We fished, we hiked, we white-water rafted, and enjoyed the best of the high country. The last day that they were here they helped me with the stream. Jimmy, the water snake came to pay a visit to Harry while he was moving rocks, and he was unperturbed by him and just said hello.

"There's a snake in the water and I don't even care," Harry said proudly.

We are extremely careful identifying snakes but know this snake as "Jimmy, the water snake." The water snakes are nonpoisonous but are predators for small prey in the water. The snake always comes when I move rocks since I disturb the insects and small minnows and do half the work for him to have lunch. But we were building diverters and trying to eliminate dead spots in water flow, so we were disturbing the water and Jimmy showed up. I showed them how to place the stones to help direct the current positively and explained to them that it does matter where you place every rock and how it affects the entire system. Margaret Annie oversaw and headed up the water snake hunting department.

They understand the water. Even in their play and in the stream walking and crashing sand and rocks, they were good stewards of the stream and were kind as they traversed the water acting as new explorers. It was wonderful to watch and realize that these four little feet walked the same water that countless feet of other children walked upstream in the water connecting to life; that the water they are touching is struggling to make its way downstream to reach the river, to reach the ocean and to touch other lives in its connectivity.

This is a living experiment to sustain constant water flow since the stream width is narrow and the volume exceedingly small, so the diverters and the cross vanes are small but are effective. The cross vanes have helped reduce the erosion and redirect water flow to the center but allow the constant flow of water through them. This method of water control is contrary to building a dam which does not allow controlled water flow through and does not direct flow to the center. A dam restricts the flow of water, cutting off communication upstream. Many people still build dams to block off water, to deepen areas in sections to use as swimming holes. Inadvertently this can cause stagnant pools with excessive silt built up.

I spotted a black mink patrolling the banks. It is a rarity here, and additionally since they are nocturnal animals it is rare to see them in the day. It means that there is a high probability that there is a food source there now. It means that the ecosystem is beginning to restore from the microbes to the nymphs, to the crayfish, to the minnows, to the chubs, to the small trout, to the water snakes to the mink. He is a vicious predator and I hope he does not get too comfortable here.

7-1-22

Harry and I worked the stream in the next small area upstream of the bridge and saw small six to eight inches fish and Jimmy the small water snake. We were deepening this area right before the short falls near a huge boulder on the bank. We were trying to redirect the still water, elevate the dead water, and remove silt while deepening and raising the water level. Margaret walked upstream and saw Bobby the huge water snake. Harry walked a few yards ahead of me upstream and I looked up and saw him frozen, standing as still as a column and quiet as a church mouse. My first reaction was I needed to fly to his rescue and thought the worst. He then said in a lower voice I barely heard, "Papa, look!" he pointed. He was standing five feet from a baby fawn curled up motionless on a rock in the middle of the stream.

The rock is an island with large grass growing from it three feet tall. The boulder is around six feet in diameter. The little fawn, curled up in a tight ball, hid in that clump of warm tall grass atop the boulder. A miracle of nature to see the grass growing atop the boulder but enough dirt has accumulated on the rock to cultivate this plant. The wonderful tall green grass swaying gently was hiding, at its base, the baby fawn, brown with dark spots along its back laying perfectly camouflaged. As Harry went closer it perked up its tiny ears, opened its huge brown eyes, staring directly at Harry but did not move a muscle. I am sure the little fawn was under strict orders from mom to remain perfectly still regardless of what happened. And so, we carefully worked and walked around hoping not to disturb; her eyes grew wider, but she did not move. That night before the temperature dropped to the low fifties and I am sure the rock was a wonderful place to rest and hide and take full advantage of the sun pelting the rock all day then dissipating the heat slowly through the night. The grass covered boulder was a heated bed mat, hiding spot for the fawn and a beautiful gift for Harry and me and one I hope he remembers.

7-8-22

These last few days have been excruciatingly difficult as I am continually chasing the lack of water in the stream. Rainfall continues to be scarce and when it does occur it comes in half inch increments. The water volume reduced dramatically. It is easier to work the stream now because I have ready access to the shallow bottom. If I can achieve steady water flow, even at a minimal level, at the worst and driest condition it will only be better when the rain fuels its vibrant energy. When the water is at its lowest, as it is now, I resurvey the design and the stream's desired current pattern and attempt to compensate by modifying each boulder, each drop, each curve, every diverter, every cross vein and every move to suit the drop in water. My problem is I am chasing the constant retraction of stream and water and am hungry for rain to show me where I have succeeded and failed. It is in these situations where I must have faith in how the stream guides me since the water gives us no clues.

I am in a constant battle with the withdrawal of the stream and the shrinking of my main tool, the water. I also must be constantly vigilant and attempt to project, visualize, and remember what the stream will be when it rains again, and additionally how it reacts when it floods. It is impossible to fully predict. But as an architect I do the same impossible task to visualize and plan what a structure will be in sun, wind, rain, snow, and extreme temperature changes; interpret uses and allow for changes over time. Then I attempt to elevate the work to art. It is never perfect but a practice that attempts to solve most of the problems and elevates perception. I still believe, after forty years, that it is simple magic. I have told students, if we strive to design and anticipate solving ninety percent of all the issues, and struggle to elevate solutions to art; the remaining ten percent oftentimes surprises us with magic.

Lately even with this lack of rain, the water temperature is at sixty-five degrees. This is borderline maximum upper temperature, to sustain for adult brookies, but not young ones. Rainbow and brown trout can survive in water of higher temperature.

7-9-22

It rained one inch in six hours and the stream reacted wonderfully. The cross veins diverted water, the diverters rerouted water, the faster more vibrant current washed silt away exposing gravel bottom. But I am not satisfied with the variation in the stream depths throughout and will focus on that part of the puzzle next. The upper section and lower sections are working well and simply need depth adjustments but the lower section directly upstream of the bridge is horrible. But while observing the increased water flow, I may have stumbled upon an answer to work that section next. Any perceived solution is always an educated guess, but that is today's effort. This area has been problematic and has required thoughtful consideration since I dismantled the dam just fifty feet downstream from the bridge. The rain has caused another delay in finishing the steps. Unfortunately, I must have two teeth pulled and there is a constant ache, but I must get to the stream.

Overnight a large boulder, eight feet across, decided to roll into the stream from its precarious perch on the steep bank along the roadside. I have been watching this rock for a year, frozen and stuck on the almost vertical bank looking like it's a dead fall trap with a hidden trigger. It dropped eight feet to the stream and settled close to the bank edge. And there it will stay. There is still over ten feet of buffer between the road, fifteen feet above the stream and the stream bank, and this rock appears to have no structural impact on the road. I placed a courtesy call to DOT Watauga County and discussed the fallen rock. They returned the call.

"Hello, this is Mark."

"Is this Mark?"

"Hello, yes this is Mark Wright, who is this please?"

"Mr. Wright, this is Lester from DOT, howudoin'?"

"Hello Lester, I am livin' the life, my friend, there are no bad days."

"Good, good. I'm callin' 'bout some boulder on a road?"

"Yes, not in the road, it fell from the bank. I have a large boulder that fell from the roadside into a stream, and I don't believe it is causing a structural problem, but I just wanted to discuss it with you. I'm not asking you to remove the boulder from the stream and I can go ahead and get twenty tons of rip rap ordered and put it behind the boulder up the bank to help stop any erosion and sediment bleeding into the stream but I'm checking with you first."

"Well, Mr. Wright, to be honest with you, we won't move it from the stream and anything we do on the road is months out at best."

"Lester, I figured as much, and all I want to do is get some stone up the bank and place a few plants in the right-of-way to stop the sediment and erosion. So, I'll just go ahead and thanks for the call."

"Yes sir, that'll be fine. You have a good day now."

They are not concerned about the boulder and expressed how busy they were this season, and it would be months before they can even get here to look at the road. My concern is the sediment that will migrate into the stream from the exposed bank and erosion that will occur to the remaining bank below the road. The boulder and mother nature have made a bold and clear statement about changing the stream's edge at that point. As a result, the stream will now be eight or so feet narrower at this area and will force the water to develop a revised dynamic dance around this new family member who was determined to be participating in the water and not simply on the side waiting for a deluge.

7-11-22

While walking the lower stream section, viewing it from above on the bridge, from above via the second-floor window of the cottage, and from under the bridge I thought deeply about the section of water. I had an epiphany about this center section of the run where I had been frustrated and unable to formulate solutions to the enormous issues. This area is located directly south of the cottage, and it seems the most disturbed by development. During the construction of the cottage and the bridge, modifications to the stream in this area have led to many issues that are difficult to resolve. But it came to me how to repair it, at least temporarily, and let it heal for a while. After listening to the water and observing the current, shape, and depth for hours I discovered a simple solution involving rerouting the water and again narrowing the width to increase the flow. It came to me after much deliberation and devoted listening to the water. There is a story I believe Joe Campbell told years ago.

> *A Zen master was to deliver a sermon to his pupils. He walked from the main hall of the temple through the forest down to the flowing stream as the students followed. They all stopped next to the stream and sat quietly waiting for the master to deliver the sermon. With nature surrounding them while they sat in silence, the cascading water of the stream was the only sound they heard. After thirty minutes the master stood and said, "The sermon has been delivered."*

Margaret Annie and Harry…siblings having a
private take on their labors.

The stream water temperature is around sixty-five degrees, so I am
wet wading. This means I forego waders and only use the boots.
The initial rush from the cool water around my feet instantly
informs me that the water temperature is not warmed to a deadly
temperature. The cascades and runs that I have developed breathe
oxygen into the water as a giant dynamic cooling chain assisting
the flora in cooling the water. A simple pleasure consumes me
when the water, now at its lowest level, covers the top of my
boots and embraces my shin and in some places my knee. This
may seem mundane, but it shows that the water level is at least
eight inches in its worst-case season when no rain has occurred,
and it is staying cool in the hottest month. I will accept the small
pleasures here, celebrate for two minutes, which relieves the

weight from the work since the task is overwhelming me as I chase the depleting current preparing for rain.

I worked on the area at the falls near the bridge to be less dramatic, stair stepping the elevation change and making it more conducive to fish traffic. The volume of the water is still the same, only the velocity decreased. So, now small fish can make the journey more easily upstream through the newly developed channel. I built a short cross vein fifty yards downstream directing the stream energy to the center but also raising the water level in this area. I deepened the area and deposited the rocks and sand on the veins. This should provide a deep holding spot fed by the accelerated water flow at the falls area.

As I was working, I looked up and my friend Bobby, the larger water snake, returned. He startled me and I never get used to his surprise stealthy appearance while I'm working. As I turn over the rocks and silt, it disturbs the small critters and nymphs which in turn draws the smaller fish waiting to feed. As I work the predator Bobby waits and watches patiently for unsuspecting minnows. Suddenly, I looked up and he had a two-inch trout in his mouth sideways. I could not get the camera fast enough and he kept moving out of the water to a sunny, level rock with the prize in his mouth secured with gripping serrated teeth. For a few moments, the small fish struggled, flipping, and shaking, but Bobby held tight. Then as the fish slowed its writhing and the water's energy left its small body, Bobby instinctively knowing it was time, flipped the fish around. Holding it headfirst, it seemed as if the small fish swam into the snake's body and Bobby swallowed it before I could blink. He waited for only thirty seconds on the warm flat rock before being off again to hunt. I was amazed and thought that he needed to rest and digest his catch as a snake, but this was contrary to that thought, and he was ready to fight again. Witnessing this creature bound to the earth but hunting in fluid waters, drawing life from a creature bound to the water was mesmerizing and a brilliant symbolic gift.

7-12-22

The forecast called for heavy rain beginning at 10:00 am. I did not want to start and then stop the work, so I took my cup of tea and went surveying the conditions of the lower stream area. I had on my rubber boots so at least I could walk in certain areas of the stream easily and protected. The lower area stream is denser with trees that come right to the stream edge in several areas. This provides enormous shade and cover in this area, and the air temperature drops at least ten degrees. I had done some work here in preparation to come back and tune it. Today I was not prepared with my partner the shovel and pick but could not resist working until the rain began. So, I began moving boulders and rocks from the bottom to help redirect and displace flow. It never did rain and I worked until 2:00 p.m. then stopped for an hour lunch and resumed at 3:00 p.m. and worked until 7:00 p.m.

I worked on the lower section of the stream where I am sure I have inadvertently affected the flow here from work upstream. Again, the butterfly effect in practice. I am cleaning up the tumbled boulders here and assisting the stream to recenter and desilt. This is more untouched by development and has only the access road on one side but only a few structures anywhere all the way to the river. Still, the stream suffers the same issues due to the years of deposits from upstream development and road runoff. Who knows how long these boulders have been here? But there are concrete and asphalt remnants of the old bridge washed downstream in '05, time stamping the moment when the stream changed in our lifetime. Massive pieces of concrete and asphalt, claimed by the stream are now permanent fixtures. Huge boulders could have been placed when the initial road was built, others tumbled by the '05 hurricane floods, and still others tossed recently by last year's deluge, and still others may have been here since time carved the stream.

As I looked up, I saw a small black mink sashaying down the stream. He jumped in the water popped up on the bank, scurried over a rock, slithered under a boulder, and cocked its head curiously. There was no fear, only blatant curiosity, and if possible, an impish smile expressed on its whiskered face. It was making its way to my lunch bag setting on shore. And I yelled, "Git! Go on now, that is not yours." So, I tossed a rock toward the critter, and it playfully and humorously showed me and chased the rock. I assume I was not as interesting as it originally thought, and it scurried up the bank hill deep into eighteen-inch-high grasses. I could follow the path of the moving grass and every now and then could see it pop its head above sniffing, further downstream maybe fifteen yards. It was serious, and it looked as if it had caught a mouse, shrew, or chipmunk, and was carrying it proudly further downstream. He is a vicious predator who sometimes kills for sport as a serial killer and not for food. I'm concerned that he is happy about the increase in life in the stream and is anticipating a coming buffet. He is part of the system, but the small fish and other wildlife do not stand a chance against him. The Hansens duck gave birth to a brood of late ducklings, twelve in all. Now they have only eight left and we suspect the mink, as those small babies are easy pickings for the brute.

I was moving rocks and thinking of my second job as a young architect and my second two bosses. Both came from money and their parents were hard working construction people who made their fortunes in the Cincinnati and Cleveland areas. One of them, Larry was more business oriented, and the other younger partner, Mike, technical, so their relationship was copacetic and successful. One day I was working on a presentation for an office building and in those days, we hand drew original large ink drawings later printed for the presentation. I had finalized the design and was supposed to finish the drawing then have it shipped up to Larry in Cincinnati so he could give the presentation later that evening at around seven o'clock. Early that morning, I was finalizing the rendering and an entire cup of tea spilled onto the drawing washing down the sheet in a blur of liquid. Everyone went into a panic. But I calmly called Larry and told him what had happened. He said, "Mark, can you get it redone by 5:00 p.m. and meet in Cincy at 7:00 p.m. and I'll just use the original for the presentation mounted to a foam core board." "Yes sir," I said. And with post haste completed the drawing and met Larry at a restaurant in Cincinnati at 6:45 p.m.. With inward reflection, the stream draws continuous filed images from my collective memory out into the water exposing them to the cooling waters and, this time, with smiles and grateful memories of those two men, washes them downstream.

7-19-22

Yesterday it rained one and a quarter inch and it barely affected the stream and the structures held well. This rain brought the stream to an acceptable water level flowing beautifully. The lack of rain has caused the stream to run grey with limestone dust from the gravel road run off above the stream level. This subsides after six to eight hours, and the stream becomes clear.

The stream level is fickle and drops half to one inch over the next twenty-four hours if there is no additional rainfall. So having the optimum depth to maintain a healthy environment with continuous water flowing is a challenge.

This week there has been a global heat wave where Britain is seeing temperatures at 104 degrees and here in the mountains the temperature is ninety with ninety-four percent humidity. The most alarming issue here is the temperature does not drop during the night and appears to be eight to ten degrees warmer than a year ago on average, according to my utility bill tracker. Then, I could sleep with an open window as the temperature always dropped below sixty degrees at night. Now it does not drop below seventy degrees and I need to run the mini split system to cool the upstairs bedroom at nighttime.

This is troubling because it affects the stream temperature and evaporation cycle. Even if it can maintain a water temperature of sixty-five degrees, the air temperature is above eighty degrees and with the sun and any breeze accelerates evaporation. As a result I am working constantly, considering the air temperatures and any air movement. I am addressing this phenomenon by decreasing the stream width thus reducing the surface area and thus evaporative surface area and trying to increase the plant life immediately adjacent to the stream. But to my dismay, another significant issue is, I have no control over upstream water flow or stream configuration. In extreme rainy conditions, I receive the accumulation of all upstream rain which is often detrimental causing extreme flooding and in the dry season I'm fortunate to be in the lower section of the stream since I receive the accumulations of all upstream runoff helping the water level, a double-edged sword.

Harry and Margaret Annie surveying the banks for anything
that could impede the flow.

Laurel Creek after the rain.

Chapter XIV

I had two teeth pulled yesterday and a bone graft. It was not my best day. It rained and the stream looks good, but I will need to adjust part of the upper section tomorrow if I feel better and the pain has subsided—we will see. Otherwise, I will rest, plan, and try to behave as the doctor has ordered. Warned about tearing my stitches loose by everyone, I rest, and I am meditating. I begin to write and fall prey to those remaining useless negative fragments of my memory, demons, and the like, which attempt to pierce the joyful calm of the mountains and stream. They appear from behind the clouds of recollection like a fiery dragon scorching the stillness and sneaking upon me in a weakened hour. The stream has not yet quenched these last lingering smoldering coals but beckons me to use her soothing waters in concert with the mystical healing souls of my children and my grandfather, to snuff them out and wash them downstream. So, after spewing these images on pages, purging the darker halls of memory, I assembled the papers, wadded each page into a ball, placed them in a yellow porcelain bowl, sat on the porch and with a solemn prayer set them afire.

The slight flame and modest smoke rose drifting away on the mountain breeze. The ashes accumulated in the bowl, and I carried them down to the lower section of the stream, with a slow deliberate movement, and with the same reverence I showed as a child while carrying the makings for the Eucharistic sacrament up the center aisle of the church to meet the priest at the front altar. I squatted down at the edge of the bank, slowly dipping the bowl, and I watched the ash drift away as I lowered the bowl in the water. I felt the pain from centuries of energy vampires purge from my blood; watching the ashes floating quietly like Harry's leaf boats downstream in the bosom of the stream, over rocks, boulders, and dissolving and disappearing; absorbed by the healing waters. A long-exhaled breath covered me; a lift of spirit embraced me; a freedom of soul held me with tears as I let go. Again, I profoundly thank the stream.

7-25-23

What I have not worked needs work, what I worked slightly needs work, and where I have been working hard needs work, so I would say overall it's successful. The main points of the structure are holding wonderfully. The stream bank containment works and the overflow areas for flooding works, allowing excess water from the main channel to slowly spread and dissipate energy. The water receded quickly in the July heat, so I could work yesterday and tune areas. The modified deflector veins are the second-best answer to this stream structure, along with reducing the actual stream width since water flow is unpredictable and low under normal conditions. The idea of breaking the stream up into multiple working sections and narrowing the width of the main channel is the most productive way of coaxing the water to work well; to keep water flowing, to manage progress, and the silt washes down exposing a beautiful intricate gravel bottom.

July's water level had been dismal, and then came the flood waters. It rained one inch in eight hours and the stream worked swimmingly. The stream boundary holds during the flooding and the reshaped riparian area takes the overflow well absorbing the additional discharge. There is a precarious balance between the depth, the width and water velocity with this limited water flow. If I develop areas too deep or too wide for too long a run, it simply becomes a stagnant pool with silt build up. It is a tough line to walk, but again I must suggest ideas to the stream, try them out and see how she reacts. Global warming and the flash flooding is real. St Louis is under water from monsoon rains they have never seen. Boone just flooded from extreme rain yesterday and here, just twenty miles downstream there is below normal rainfall.

It appears with the amount of water flow that the structures are most efficient when breaking the stream into smaller lengths of runs between fifty to sixty feet using riffles, drops, and varying stream width. Make no mistake, there is water flow now and a defined channel where last year there was only a trickle across a flat plane and pebbles, and one deep section over the entire stream. There is life, from insects to mammals, now in abundance and seen easily moving in the stream. Yet, my work has just begun to affect change and I continually attempt to prepare the stream for extreme conditions without hurting the success of the current work. And as with any attempt at creating art, there is a moment when we must stand back and assess the work product and make the decision, Is there anything I can add, subtract or change, that will make a profound difference, or am I simply feeding my ego, attempting to reach some inaccessible perfection? That is a difficult and precarious moment standing on the precipice reflecting on the stream work as it reflects me; and I realize nature is the perfection and I am but a tool assisting it with the mystic motions, sitting grateful in her bosom to simply play some small role.

7-29-22

I have been having problems with the wide flatter area just east and upstream from the bridge and have not been able to solve the issues here. Yesterday I decided to attempt a bold move after studying the stream and water flow for hours and contemplating the location and interrelationships of the existing larger boulders. I will narrow this portion down, introduce a hard curve in the bank structure, connect the dots of existing large boulders, utilize a series of diverters, and bend the stream back again. There is a huge boulder that was the first mark to hit, and I begin the work there. I will use one side of the boulder as the main stream side channel, and the other side becomes landside and part of the riparian area sloping up to the higher bank, instead of the full boulder encircled by water. The bank will slope up from the boulder, and in most conditions the stream flows around it to one side while during a flood it should overflow like any other deflector and help recenter the stream. The fundamental action here is, I did not build a new deflector, but instead used the existing boulders in partnership to naturally curve the stream and bend the water. I will be able to repeat this design several times along this stretch of stream, and it seems as if I am simply helping the stream redirect water as it has always done. We will see.

8-3-22

I drove to pick up the children to spend a few days with me in the mountains. Their mother drove them halfway and we met in Pikeville, KY. As we were leaving the sky began to darken directly over our route. The rain began. Margaret Annie sat in the front seat and Harry slept in the back seat as we drove. The rain came in buckets and the visibility was horrible. We often encountered flooded highways and standing water. This made for a tenuous trip. Finally, after leaving the Kentucky mountains the rain subsided and Margaret was hungry. I told her only a small snack because we were going to have Indian food for dinner. We stopped, woke Harry and they got a small snack for the road. Margaret resumed her front seat position and Harry immediately fell asleep again in the back seat.

I called ahead for Indian food, and we drove directly there to pick up dinner, then drove off through the city of Boone. We made it to main street, downtown when Harry woke up and said, "Papa, I think I need to stop at a restroom." I said, "Harry, we are going to be home in 10 minutes can you hold it." The words barely left my mouth when Harry erupted and vomited on the back seat of the car and kept it up for an unimaginable amount of time. The timing was perfect and ironic since my sense of taste and smell just returned from my COVID-19 experience. Margaret Annie, being a sympathetic vomiter was gagging theatrically in the front passenger seat.

I pulled into the first Baptist church of Boone parking lot and saw that Harry was alright, gave him water and began to clean up the damage the best I could with a roll of paper towels and water I always carry in the car for just these types of emergencies. Harry got out of the car and began directing my efforts saying, "I told you I needed to stop," which was incredibly helpful while I was cleaning the back seat of the car. Margaret Annie got out gagging and screaming, and I was frantically cleaning. I politely and sarcastically asked him if he could be a bit more specific next time before he cuts lose so we know what is coming and be preemptive. He said, "I think I can manage that, Papa, but again, I did tell you I needed to stop."

After the event Harry was fine, chipper, energized, and hungry as if nothing had happened. He expelled the demon. Margaret was, well, still dramatically sympathetic since the car carried the overwhelming aroma of fresh vomit and the Indian food we had just picked up.

We made it home, across the bridge, across the smiling stream and up to the house. I asked the children to help me with the luggage and the food up the rear steps to the second-floor kitchen. Margaret Annie went up first as I was giving Harry bags to carry. He went on. As I was getting the remaining bags I heard a scream from Harry, "Wasps, wasps, wasps, Papa!" I ran up the steps, frantically grabbed Harry, covering him with my left arm and moved him down the steps away from the swarm, losing my glasses in the mayhem. Margaret said, "Papa, it looked like you were flying with Harry, and I don't think you touched the last 5 steps." I don't remember, all the while being stung repeatedly as I covered him. There was a nest of yellow jackets under the steps, that Margaret Annie disturbed, and poor Harry caught the brunt of their anger. Harry was stung several times on his leg, and I was stung multiple times on my arm and ear. After dealing with the invaders with spray foam, and tending to Harry's stings, the heavy rain during the drive and the incident at the church, we sat down for a welcomed uneventful quiet dinner and a movie. The next day we searched unsuccessfully for my missing glasses. I suspect the fleeing yellow jackets stole and transported my spectacles away as a cruel joke. The rest of the weekend was wonderful. We hiked, fished, played in the stream, and around a campfire shared a jocular retelling of the rain, the vomit trip, yellow jackets, and stories from the weekend.

At The Window With Anticipation
Pen, ink, pencil and gesso on paper
Mark T. Wright

8-6-22

I drove Margaret Annie and Harry back yesterday. Today, I waded in the stream working to console the insufferable emptiness that I feel each time the children leave, lamenting as gravity seems like an unyielding suction, all the heavier tugging down on my body. But in the stream I hear the contagious sound of their laughter always echoing off these mountains, and slowly I fill, lifting with joyous energy, and I am bursting with priceless memories until I see them again. I continued to work on the area just upstream from the bridge, and finally believe I have begun to resolve this area ; the water flow is moving well. I have cleared the area around four boulders and deepened these areas adjacent to the bridge. My work focus is on simplification, clarity of details at this point, and on incremental and small successes. There is still much work to do to refine the areas with depth, water flow, and stream width; and then there is the entire development of the landscaping of the riparian area and soil replacement that must come later. Just from the work performed, the riparian area has migrated down assisting in the flood and erosion control. I am anxious, but all in good time.

July has been hot and dry but August, according to the *Farmers' Almanac* is supposed to have average to above average rainfall. Last September, we had the remnants of hurricanes come through the high country and dump enormous amounts of water in brief time periods. In a two-day period there was one inch of rainfall in the first twenty-four hours; then another three inches overnight, and the stream became flooded. I am anxious to witness something like that event again and observe how the stream reacts with the work completed. This is a humorous rhetorical statement since I believe the work will never really be completed. There are spots along the bank that required fill on the upstream section to push the banks slope up to the adjacent soil levels. In a hard rain a braded stream configuration appears in the middle upstream area. Although I have defined the new stream edge and a successful main center channel here, I have not yet been able to sufficiently build the banks eroded edges up sloping from the water to the upper soil level to route the water to the center channel.

Consequently, in this section of stream, there are "two stream" channels during a flood event; the main one and a smaller one that appears closer to the bank when the stream rises and there is a parallel run adjacent to the main area. This secondary "braided" parallel run of about fifty yards still causes erosion, and this needs to be filled with stone and sloped up to the soil bank, then supplemented with earth and replanted to establish a revived riparian area. It is an overwhelming amount of work to accomplish. The problems are obvious, and the solutions are obvious in certain instances. When the stream bed floods, this area fills with water and creates a small low flowing secondary stream against the upper bank. There is no lack of work, or lack of goals, objectives, or strategies, to help move the stream to balance, just time and resources.

8-7-22

I am waiting for severe storms to move across the mountains, as predicted, and hoping it will bring heavy rain. When I evaluate the entire stream, I have about ninety percent of the bank in satisfactory condition and carved in an outlined form. Still many spots need tapering and tailoring to increase flow and stop erosion. The other spots need to be deepened and the deflector veins need shoring up and completing. The area upstream where the property begins needs attention and requires tapering of the banks from the upper soil to the water. It may be the only area where I do not have enough material in the stream to support this work properly. But overall, after a year and a half of solid challenging work, the overall ideas and effort appear to be successful and have helped the stream become alive again. The positive impact of work at this incremental level should not be understated, and as I flap my butterfly wings in the high country, maybe it affects a temperature drop in England, or helps create a thunderstorm in Africa, or an attitude change from a visitor here. This may be the largest impact; the positive manifestation of an attitudinal butterfly effect. Now that is a mouthful.

8-8-22

I was refining areas in the stream where silt still gathers, and slow flow continues. Now begins deepening the main channel from a downstream location working upstream to unhinge the rocks. The first action to accomplish is to remove the top sediment and small rocks and deposit these onto the deflector veins and deflectors as a base; then leverage the next layers of rocks, usually four to six inches from the locked bottom, and deposit in the same spot. I stop for a moment to allow the current to wash across the area to clear the sediment away to see the work. Then the next step is to lever out the eight-inch rocks with my shovel while also shoveling away the loose sediment that comes from upstream. Then the effort shifts to dislodging the larger boulders encased in the bottom and moving them up to shore up the banks. Then the routine repeats.

This is laborious and arduous. See what we have accomplished, a shovel at a time. Then the rain began. It reminded me of a story:

A master of Kyudo was preparing a demonstration for his students when a massive and violent rainstorm erupted as he was preparing to shoot. The students began to gather all the equipment to take it indoors as the rain made visibility almost impossible. Suddenly they realized the master was still going through his ceremony in preparation to shoot. They stopped as the master proceeded to draw his bow and take his first shot. The rain did not let up and no one could really see the target, but they thought they heard the arrow hit. The master went through his ceremony again in preparation for his second arrow and the rain became harder. The master drew and shot the second arrow allowing the Yumi to rotate in his hand. He stayed in his meditative state for some time after the release and by then the storm had subsided. The students came out and saw the results. The first arrow was dead center in the target and the second arrow split the first. The students stupefied with amazement could not believe what they just witnessed, not only amazing shots but during a driving rainstorm. They gathered round the master who was in quiet repose and one student asked, "Master how can you shoot in conditions like that during that horrific rain?" The master said, "There was no difference than any other time or conditions...I simply shot between the raindrops."

I worked until the storm became intolerable, and even in the August heat I became chilled, and I took shelter under one of the trees. This worked for a brief time, but then I became soaked to the bone and cold, so I moved up the bank across the clearing to the small shed for shelter. I stood inside the shed looking at the rain pouring and was happy to finally get the desperately needed drenching. The stream began to swell gently, but the storm was only a tease, and the rain stopped abruptly before it affected the water level. But any rain is a welcome event.

8-9-22

I continued the work refining the channel, moving slowly across the entire width of the upstream section from the bridge two feet of width at a time. Since I choked this portion of the stream down, the depth is working well, and it was the right decision after long study and deliberation. I never know the full impact of my work and designs until the water, stream, and nature evaluate them. But the solutions are working and solving multiple problems. Nothing is, or can be complete and one hundred percent resolved, but I believe we are on the right track working together toward achieving relative balance.

I went to survey the entire stream again, and as I was moving along the bank downstream from the bridge I was in the bush on the bank and felt a stab in my thigh and thought I hit a thorn bush. But the stab happened a second time and then it registered, I was stung again multiple times on my hand and arm as I moved some brush away. I had disturbed a huge yellow jacket nest, and these creatures are not accommodating to trespassers. Unlike bees, they can and will sting multiple times and with a vicious fury and without reservation. The area is off limits now until fall when they leave and abandon the nest. But they made it abundantly clear in the meantime that I was to stay in the stream and not to venture into their territory. They could have been a little more congenial about the whole matter, but they are determined to uphold their reputation, and I am very willing to yield.

8-28-22

I have been diligently refining the depth and width of the area above the bridge and feeling pressure to complete the work. The rainfall has been well below normal, and temperatures are above normal. I sat on the large stone in the middle of the stream and as I became settled in and motionless, life began to happen around me. Deer came closer and took no mind of me, minnows and chubs darted all around my feet, pond skimmers gathered below my feet since I caused a welcome break in the current, crawdads moved all around, and even a small salamander braved the moment and moved from rock to rock. It is necessary to stop often and see the stream and understand the actions and change in actions I have started and placed in motion. Deepening the area here has cultivated a wonderful place for life and allowed the slower controlled flow of water. There is no grander measurement of success for the work in this stream than to see these waters reinvigorated and become a cradle for life.

The hummingbirds are active and visit every plant and trumpet vine that is still blooming and producing flowers. They are preparing to fly south, but they are stopping, hovering, and they are watching me with interest. But they do stop and appear to look me in the eye before they speed off. Are they saying goodbye until the next season? Are they saying thank you for the extra syrup in the feeder? Are they inspecting the work as a superintendent of the air? Or are they, hopefully, paying a visit of affirmation that what I am doing is long overdue and acceptable to them? Or are they simply sharing their magical gifts as an encouragement for me to continue while they are away. For me, it is a sad temporary goodbye tempered with the knowledge that they usually return, and I say to them, "Just wait until you see the stream and garden next year when you return, safe travels little friend."

Does crossing Laurel Creek following a pathway up the mountain

9-5-22

Two inches of rain fell last night and the stream flooded but the stream banks held as it was planned, and overflowed where it needed after the channel reached its bank fill. Today the water level is perfect, but I know that will not last. However, it gives me hope.

9-15-22

I worked yesterday and the mountains felt like they were welcoming fall for the first time. The wind was gusting, escorting the leaves to the ground. But in one glorious case I witnessed a single determined leaf blown by the wind, tumble, twist, resist gravity, sail upward, rolling, then down, then upward again, rotating for one hundred yards west to east; darting between trees and branches, sliding by each obstacle fluidly as it was spinning. Then it shifted its flight horizontally, not dropping, but again floating, teetering back and forth stubbornly, willfully catching a ride on currents to land on the limb of a birch tree, solid and still as if it were reattached. This one special leaf seemed determined to roost on this tree after leaving its original home somewhere up the mountain. It struck a deal with the breeze to dance one last romp from tree to tree and not allow gravity to conquer it just yet.

The air was chilly, the stream colder and my waders leaked. My hands became cold for the first time this year and my socks and pants became soaked and cold. Fall was coming and the stream still needed work. Then the wind began to howl on the leading front of a storm system and to rock every tree and bush. It is amazing to watch how each plant and tree react to the wind moving; some flutter, some wave some simply bounce, some sway, in a syncopated but different timing and rhythm. They all move, but in this unpredictable beautiful dance. Each tree swayed differently from the mountain side down to the stream. The pines still holding their green needles barely swayed their main trunks. The fine needles flutter as the small branches shift gracefully relaying the movement to the main larger limbs. But the larger main trunk moves slightly after the millions of needles filter the winds. The walnut trees long and thin, with their bark resembling the flow of the stream, reaching up to eighty feet, now mostly naked, have no flutters. They swing and sway from the earth as if their main trunk were hinged about six feet above the ground. The entire tree, small, medium, and large branches sway in unison with the gusts. The red bud set with their main trunk still and the ancillary limbs sway, rock, and shutter randomly as they spread out from the main base. Some have split and are wired together as the upper sections spread away from the main trunk.

There was damage to the bank structure in various areas from someone on the lower sections of the stream moving and removing rocks to build dams. Someone attempted to tear down one of the "no trespassing" signs. I struggle to tune the stream properly over its entire length where I eliminate the sand and silt deposits. There is not enough consistent water flowing in all locations to make it harmonize completely and simultaneously. I have established a water flow and small falls by creating sections of pools even at the lowest rain cycle, but I cannot seem to coax the stream to sing in complete and constant harmony with the water. The higher water after a rain is beautiful but it fades quickly. The extreme conditions, feast, or famine, make it difficult to achieve any type of relative consistency. Additionally, often there is the destructive interference of persons walking the stream who know nothing of the water but damage the work and who instead build dams which intensify the harsh destructive conditions. I'm sure their intentions are harmless, and they do not realize the damage the dams caused. As Harry and I hike from the waterfall, every hike we stop and deconstruct every dam along the half mile trek. The warmer the weather the more traffic in the stream and the more invasion and the more dam building and the more "dam building."

The stream modifications work for the most part. Still, she teases me exposing certain efforts as follies and consistently reminding me that she and the water are in step with nature and two steps ahead of me; that she is in charge, sometimes a victim sometimes a friend, but always part of nature and its unpredictable unyielding forces. And I'm still a neophyte even after more than three thousand two hundred hours working in the stream.

Over near the Cove Creek general store, the major reconstruction work on a part of the stream continues with heavy equipment. The banks are stabilized below the stream edges with stones the size of Buicks and the channel is being dredged out deeper and the bank slopes up from the stone Buicks at forty-five degrees where I am assuming there will be plants and the newly constructed riparian area. This is a consistent and effective solution to the erosion of the banks, but it is still leaving the edges straight and sterile. I read that this is a major ongoing effort in connection with the University of North Carolina and the Resource Institute and that they have previously worked on an upper section of the Stream years ago. It appears to be effective. But it is not art.

At times I feel defeated and overwhelmed at the Herculean task. The work is slow and unforgiving, arduous and often frustrating, and my body bends from the strain. I will need to get back to working on the steps and the house and carriage house soon before winter sets in. What I have accomplished is all that I can accomplish.

9-17-22

I worked yesterday, now the fifth day in a row, tweaking the stream depth and flow. There has been no rain for five days and it looks like no rainfall expected for another five days, so it will be interesting to see if the stream maintains consistent water flow through the drought. I moved boulders the size of coffee tables. Someday, I will not be able to do this work as age will catch up with me no matter how fast I run from it. I am aware that I cannot move a boulder where it does not want to go, but in some cases these stones may have held submerged for a hundred years and now are allowed to breathe by my hand.

These boulders often tease me and barely poke their heads above the stream bottom just being nosey and wanting to see what is transpiring. Others are saying, "It's my turn," and I make every attempt to hear them. Then we had a serious discussion about where they want to go. I try to accommodate them in every case, after all it is their world. As with any entity they often change their mind and after a hard rain they shift and move to other locations despite my most insistent efforts. The water moves them but who decides when, where, and how? Are the rocks and boulders leaping on the current to ride to another location or are they a victim of the water and moved or moving without provocation?

The sand, rocks, and boulders constantly converse with the water as part of the stream family. Their conversations linger long after I leave the water and they decide whether their location is adequate and agreed to by the rock, the stream, and the water. They have been having discussions like this since creation, but now I have them talking differently to see if they remember of the time when they conversed before man intervened. We then have another exchange debating the current (pun intended) conditions, their new location and position. Eventually we come to an agreement until the next deluge. Then a new dialogue surfaces. It is not for reasons of nostalgia to spark a new conversation about their history, but to discuss new alternatives to achieve balance. You cannot make sense of where you are going if you don't know where you've been. Occasionally, I believe I feel the stream and the water, rocks, and boulders, trees and animals reminisce and indulge with recollections of the past.

These moments I embrace and acknowledge but insist we all focus on the present and understand that all changes and all events, good and bad, have led us on these converging paths independently and as a collective. Every house built, every road reconstructed, every rain, every flood, every wisp of the salamander tale, every swift flip of the crawdads swimmerets, every smoothing of every stone by the grace of the water, every fallen tree limb lodged along the bank with clogging temporary organic leaves filtering the stream, every pebble perfectly tossed exposing its wet underbelly, every vehicle traversing the gravel road, every foot pressing down stirring silt, every breeze exhaling across the stream since the first trickle of water that brought us together are all connected and have had an impact. And now I'm the newest factor inserted into the complex equation, well-intentioned, overzealous, hardworking, and with overwhelming desire to become part of this stream community to help achieve balance.

The original work in certain sections was a necessary place holder to help train and identify the boundaries of the stream during high and low water. And now I disassemble areas after studying where the high-water marks are and taper the slopes more gently. Most people would not immediately understand the strategy, but it asked the stream to help, to evolve, and to gently ease into a new form. It is like building braces temporarily adjusting the stream teeth. The water has begun to respond, And the stream has held its form, and the deluge is more controlled limiting its destruction. As I deepened sections, built deflectors, and routed the stream in a meandering pattern, the water now takes on a different attitude during a storm. The water contained by the stream edges helps control its destructive energy, allowing the water to dissipate into designated areas. The water seemed compliant and even satisfied by having a new intended boundary. It is as if the water secretly desires help, and with a more controlled structure takes solace in the guided movement. I have no illusion of taming this water-beast in the event of horrific rains and catastrophic flooding. But when the heavy rains come, so far up to two inches in twenty -four hours, the stream reacts better in a more controlled fashion limiting the thievery of soil and saving the precious birch trees along the banks. The stream community appears to be working in unison toward a balance. It just may have been searching for a conductor.

I also moved boulders after observing the gathering of silt behind them. I moved these stones to increase and direct the water flow to wash these silted areas out and expose a gravel bottom. This solution is not effective everywhere when the stream is at its normal to low flow rate, but eliminating as many silted areas as possible at lower water levels will only achieve a healthier stream at higher water levels. If left alone the silt could continuously gather and develop into large sand bars bringing the stream back to an unbalanced state. Although this is normal, to some degree, and some silt will normally be washed on during higher water levels and floods, it is best to start with the elimination of this sediment where possible and try to maintain an exposed gravel bottom.

9-24-22

The air has changed, and the trees are giving up the last of their summer dress. It always has seemed strange to me how the fall winds undress the trees for winter. But the wind coming from the northwest is chilled and harsher now, and when it gusts it draws its strength from atop the mountains releasing the leaves in explosive bundles, like thousands of fluttering golden snowflakes falling slowly. The leaves fall further in the mountains. They float for a longer duration before hitting the lower ground and at the stream. I find it hard to believe they are no longer alive. I believe they are simply in transition exposing life through their mystic actions, and sky, and water. As I stand amidst these almost weightless objects, I think of thousands of years and the thousands of hearts that have floated among these mountains like these leaves, and the multiple hearts I had floating before the children entered my life. Those many wayward hearts of mine were wistful, broken, joyful, grateful, pierced, and torn, fragmented, and weighted. Now they are being slowly forged into a single heart magically floating lighter, with miraculous aid from the children, the stream, the water, and the high country.

Yesterday I worked at the upper section of the stream at the edge of the property trying to refine the initial flow of water over a small fall. The work went well but today I feel exhausted after the fifth day in a row of lifting boulders. My exhaustion and soreness are in direct relation to the number of large boulders I moved the day before, as if that would not be obvious. There is no way to measure the work, as each portion of the stream needs a different approach and solution to achieve a natural balance. Most are approaching a balanced form now, except for a continuous problem area upstream from the bridge around a huge boulder. I cannot seem to solve this condition satisfactorily regardless of the different solutions I attempted. I must rethink this entire area again. But this run of water has always been an issue. With complicated geometry, obstacles, and elevation changes, it is the most visible section of water from the house and that adds to the obsession to "get it right."

At this point I am reinforcing areas that I have already built. I partially solved one area upstream where a braid of water shows during a hard rain. I have built this bank area up with stones and sloped it back to the water from the grassy area. And as with every other condition I have used the stone from the stream bottom to build up the edges and drop the center channel bottom working for that equilibrium. This area still requires work and fill, but I am looking forward to hard rain. My intuition is that the solution is correct, but the degree of success is always in question until the rain comes with the deluge.

I am confident it will hold up to two inches of rainfall overnight, without damage, but the test would be if there is more rainfall in a shorter period. It is critical to know and witness the stream's extremes so I can further plan for future landscaping and make plans to rebuild the riparian area over top of the stone. The layers are important, and patience is paramount. I need to develop a system to measure the work and note the conditions of the stream as they change. The first step is to document the stream as I now have as the changed baseline. I have hundreds of sketches documenting the plans I've executed. I have hundreds of photographs and videos showing the various conditions of the stream overtime. The drawings change continuously and serve as a chart of evolution for the work. I still need a more detailed overall survey for the entire stream, and I'm working on it daily.

There is an urgency to complete as much work as possible before winter before I am forced to stop this year. Any entity existing in the stream has a life contract to be here. They will be a part of the stream, the land, the children's life, and my life to enjoy and learn from. Their lives are a part of this journey and the ultimate test if I have done my part well to revive the stream. They will let me know.

9-26-22

It has rained the last two days, off and on, with one half inch of rain the first day and three quarters of an inch of rain in the last 8 hours. Work has stopped temporarily.

10-9-22

Hurricane Ian devastated Florida last week and made its way northwest before traveling back northeast. It came through the mountains and added two and a half inches of rain in twelve hours on the stream. The water level rose, and the stream overflowed its banks, but the structures held. The air temperature has dropped finally with nighttime lows in the mid-forties, and the water temperature is maintaining between fifty to sixty degrees in the sunniest sections of the stream. These are perfect conditions for trout. I have been repairing and reinforcing any areas damaged by the flood but will never be able to anticipate the worst conditions. I am continually clearing, refining, and deepening areas. The storm last week stimulated the stubborn gnats for their last swarming fall hurrah. But the other life is beginning to leave for the winter. The small fish have moved and so has Bobbie and Jimmy. The crawdads have thinned, and the salamanders seemed to have moved to their brumation homes for the winter. The mink still prowls the banks, and it seems he knows that life has returned to the stream. The conditions are right for fish life to flourish, and he is vigilant. He is primarily nocturnal but has shown his face in the early evening, so I do know his routine and course. The mink will eat every fish in this stream and will sometimes kill the prey and not eat it. The trout do not stand a chance against him and the heron.

The children and my brother and sister-in-law are coming down next week. I hope these mountains produce mystical and magical memories for Harry and Margaret Annie. It is utterly unique in every way from witnessing the stream restoration, to the small life and fish returning to the stream. At the very least it will be an informative book report for Margaret Annie and Harry when they get back to school.

Hand crafted steps from the house down a
steep slope to the stream.

10-15-22

Leaves fall on the water and those that do not float downstream sink, and show an amazing, phenomenal action in deeper areas. In multiple spots the leaves accumulate in underwater piles on the bottom of the stream, quiet and still while the current at the surface is moving above them. It is a clear example of how in just two feet of water the surface current may be complex, active, and completely different than what is going on at the stream bottom. The amazing fall leaves cover the stone banks with a gorgeous multicolor blanket as the stones peak through occasionally. Other leaves drop in the water, float for a while, then sink, squeezed, and suctioned tight against the rocks and become dams. I rethink the entire shape of the stream based on information from the leaf deposits. If we are still and watch this organic debris carefully, it tells the full story of underwater currents and adds to the translation of the complex stream language.

10-17-22

My brother Sam and his wife Patty came up from Florida to see the children who came down yesterday. The house was full and opened its arms welcoming the company. They all were here to see each other but also to see the progress of the stream and I hope to share the unique energy of the mountains. This is the first time they are together here in the house in the mountains. The anticipation for me was greatest, as everyone else did not know what to expect. We all had breakfast and talked about what was about to happen. The days were perfect, sunny, and about sixty degrees. Any work on the stream stopped and was going to continue after they all left, or not at all.

We all talked about what it meant to have life back in the stream, the problem of keeping it here, predators eating the fish, and what is next. We talked about the importance of healthy water, what it took for me to get the stream in the conditions to support life again, and what it will take to maintain it. My brother and I reminisced about our childhood growing up in the city then the suburbs in the seventies, his older two children, how our life and realities were completely different than Margaret's and Harry's, and the good fortune of having him and Patty here to know my children. We walked the stream, all hiked down to the river and back up the stream to the house looking for life as we moved.

Margaret Annie is the best spotter of any stream life regardless of size, shape or family and she can track their movement in the water. Even after our clumsy movement in the stream and any fish scattered into their holding positions camouflaged perfectly, she could find them and point them out. We all finally got out of the stream water, giving any residents peace to re-acclimate to the surroundings. We all speculated on what they were saying to each other, and hoped it was a polite conversation about being happy to be free, and discussions on how instinct would take over inside the joy of being residents of this revived water. We guessed they were a little nervous about being in this unfamiliar environment but thought they were excited about the beautiful world ahead in the stream.

10-26-22

I have been working in the stream and have seen about ten fish. I am working the upper section based on leaf deposits on the stream bottom that show direction, velocity, and complexity of water flow. I can more easily deposit rip rap from the north bank gravel road above; therefore I place stones from the stream center bottom on the opposite side of the stream on the South side bank. I stopped to rest for a minute and get a drink and was sitting motionless on a dry boulder when a large trout swam by casually in front of me. James Brown came on the radio, "I feel good," and I just danced for joy. That guy has been here hiding and I was ecstatic to see him in this section of water. It was a sign from the fish gods that this experiment may be working.

10-29-22

The sky was a brilliant red this morning as the sun tried to squeeze between the low clouds and the mountains. There was no rain, but an ominous glow pervaded the clearing near the stream. A lone deer was eating clover, blending in with the background, and until she moved her head, she was indiscernible from the grasses. The scene was deafeningly quiet and still. I am working on the steps although the stream calls to me.

11-6-22

The leaves have left the trees and the leaves that settle in the stream have been washed out by the rain two days ago. The stream is fluid and wonderful and deep at most spots, and the water is a beautiful amber tea dyed from the leaves. I see no fish and no mink. But the water and the stream are happy after the one inch of rain. I've run out of material and need to order rip rap to finish the banks.

Harry and Margaret Annie joyfully playing in the clean steam.

Laurel Creek flooded after Hurricane Nicole.

Chapter XV

Hurricane Nicole came through the area and dumped five and a half inches of rain on the stream in eighteen hours. The stream flooded wide and terrifyingly destructively. The rain made a horrible sound like a group of kettle drums pounding the metal roof, and combined with the ominous roar of the water was frightening. The stream water has risen over six feet and has tripled the width. The deluge is only thirty inches from the bottom of the bridge, and I can sense the bridge trembling with fear as I do, as the rushing water continues to rise. I can make out the main destructive flow of the water on its rampage blasting the center channel and the lesser current on the overflow along the banks. This is what is supposed to happen, but usually to a much lesser degree. I still need to raise the banks with rip rap. We will see in a few hours if structures are held in place and the overflow areas work as they are designed.

But this flood is exceptional. The center: brown, gray foaming, churning, white rapids are indifferent to the stream life. This was the worst flood since 2005. The Watauga River one-half mile away rose ten and a half feet, and the water flow was eighty times its usual flow rate completely submerging the picnic area and parking area at the Highway 321 bridge as rushing water came downstream from Blowing Rock and Boone, and Valley Cruises and Cove Creek, relentlessly punishing the area. The water seemed as if it was not going to stop rising and was on a mission to prove the hand of nature can be vicious and unpredictable.

Now three days later, the work I have done in the middle of the stream from the waterfall is not discernible. But I realized after close inspection about one half of the work is buried below twenty-four to thirty-six inches of tumble rocks and stones from far upstream. I see the outline of my old work now buried. The stream bed has risen resulting from an extreme storm. The work will resume based on the way the flood left the stream with a new reading of form and new working of the many spots. The positive irony is there is an abundance of material. This is all practice, maybe one day I will get it right.

But the flood water reacted to the new stream form and was altered by the new stream modifications. In some cases, the stream confirmed the work with her resolve as my partner and most sections remain. In other sections of the stream, the water overwhelmed our work, and it is now a transition to another form at least until the next trauma. I'm reading how this flood reacted to what remains and will work with the stream to redesign it to exist and maybe survive with less scarring. Much is left buried under two to three feet of rock so I will patiently search for the balance again in spring and summer when the water level is the lowest.

The landscape after the flood is terribly scarred, like I have never seen. Blank baron plants flattened and beat down, seem desperate, but I know spring will welcome new life and this deluge was a seventeen-year anomaly. But it is still an event, and it will help me plan for its return. The patient search and practice continue. The bridge pier rip rap washed out and I need to work on that now and simultaneously plan for the dry months of summer. There is no way to plan for this, no action that can resist this type of extreme deluge. But where is the in between? Where is the sweet spot that can survive and accommodate both? This is practice and my patient search. It continues.

I take solace in two things; the trout lived and thrived in the stream prior to the catastrophic flooding and the deluge did not destroy the work, but covered like the ash covering Pompeii, half of the structures below two feet of rock deposits. The other half of the work is either intact or improved. I see the outline of the stonework now level with the stream bottom where once it sat two feet above, and the water level is above the fill in several areas. Now the task of re-excavating the center channel, as a raving archaeologist, will begin in spring, or intermittently as a break if weather permits.

The stream and I asked the water to accept the redirection and it has, although on its own terms. The stream no longer runs straight and has collaborated with me on a compromise to change to a meandering entity, not formally as I contained it, but beautifully as it has evolved with coaxing and in partnership with the water. She is considering a negotiated evolution, and I must believe it is being kind because of my efforts to mold her into the adjusted new form. It is humbling to witness this magnificent power of the water and reassuring that it has reluctantly accepted the work. We will continue together. It is time to rest and let the stream rest while evaluating and assessing the new form, modified form, and the same form. The water still flows wonderfully. The stream survived the deluge and the non-discretion of the water and has worked out a compromise acceptable to us all. They say that fish stay put behind rocks and cover. This flood was so overwhelming I have little hope of any fish remaining in the area.

11-28-22

The children came down upholding our new two-year-old tradition of Thanksgiving dinner here in the mountains and celebrating my sixty fifth birthday and erecting the Christmas tree. Harry, drawn to the stream regardless of the weather, immediately wants to go down to build castles. This time Harry and I hiked and climbed up the back mountain deep into the woods and over the first plateau and ridge to the highest part of the upper mountain. We ascended the east slope and descended on the west slope. I believe he was happy to be going home, and when we arrived he immediately crawled under a comforter on the couch and snuggled up with a book and hot chocolate. Margaret Annie actually paid attention and became worried because we had gone for such an extended period of time. That night I helped Harry build a fire and we all roasted marshmallows. The next day we all hiked the gravel road down to the Watauga River then up the stream to the house. We never tire of the adventure.

12-12-22

Several days ago, may be the last time I worked in the stream this year. Since the water is too cold the air temperature freezes my hands when they get wet. But after the last flood and working there, I am an archeologist rediscovering my work since it was not destroyed but simply buried under three feet of rocks tossed about. The new stream geometry is a combination of what I created, what the water wants, and what the stream can tolerate—this is a beautiful thing. There is no disappointment when we know that nature's course is oftentimes violent and unpredictable but that is the predictability. So, with tools in hand, the stream, the water, and I begin the conversation again from a different and improved beginning.

12-23-22

I have not worked the stream much, due to the colder water temperatures, air temperatures and the need to work on the exterior steps. Today the air temperature is hovering at minus seven degrees, and the prediction is for it to stay frigid for several days. Snow fell overnight and is covering the area in places up to five inches. The water pump near the parking area froze, and there was no water to the house, so I drained the water heater into several large pots to make tea and to heat on the stove to wash later. I was planning to drive to Kentucky to visit the children but as of this moment the truck and car batteries are deader than a doornail and will not turn over the engine in either vehicle due to the cold. Kentucky is suffering the same cold spell with ice and snow covering the highways making it dangerous to travel. It appears the prudent thing to do is to postpone the trip one day, to be safe. A friend is bringing a new battery for me to install in the truck which I had strategically parked down the mountain, in the lower parking area, so I might escape. When the snow and ice come, I cannot make it up or down the steep sloped drive, to or from the main house at the top of the hill. My fingers are numb and cracking from touching skin to steel to remove the spent truck battery.

While I await rescue from a Good Samaritan, I sip my cup of hot and delicious tea, and even in this frigid weather I cannot resist walking the stream. The snow is shining high on my boots, the wind is howling harsh and unforgivingly, but the power of the stream will not be dampened, and it draws me to her. Water is still stubbornly moving through the veins of the stream fighting the thickening imposed by the frigid air. The enthralling sound of the cascading falls still echoes across the mountains. The water refuses to be silenced or encumbered. The stream firmly embraces the water and simply will not allow it to freeze over and be denied their combined magnificence. And as a beautiful Christmas gift, wrapped in a white blanket, they offer me the pleasure of the sound of the water and the pleasure of their company, while we wait for spring, to again experience the universal harmony in the stream existing on the underbelly of a stone rotating around the tail of a salamander.

Pristine Laurel Creek

A thriving Laurel Creek after rehabilitation.

Epilogue

A student of karate completed his years of training and came before his master to receive the highest honor and the grand symbol, the black belt.

The master asked, "What is the meaning of the black belt?"

The student replied, "It is the glorious celebration of the end of years of karate training."

The master replied, "No, come back in one year." The student left and meditated on the question for one year then came back to receive his black belt.

The master asked, "What is the meaning of the black belt?"

The student approached the master and proudly said, "It is the grand symbol for mastering the art of karate."

The master said, "No, come back in two years." The student took his leave, practiced and meditated for two years. He came back to the master again.

The master asked, "What is the meaning of the black belt?"

The student approached solemnly, knelt, bowed before the master, raised his head, and said, "It is but a token that marks the end of the beginning, and a beginning of the lifelong dedicated study and practice of the art of karate." The master handed him the black belt.

Summer is ending, and it has not rained for eight days but now the sky is darkening and there is thunder echoing across the mountains teasing me with anticipation. The clouds are quickly rushing in, dimming the day so much I need to turn a light on to work at my desk. Finally, the rain is beginning, and the sound carries through the house strongly in rhythm, like an Irish dance troupe pounding the floor of the metal roof. By the time I reached the kitchen window the storm slowed to light rain. After pouring the well water into the pot, I listened to the water boiling to make a cup of hot water, saw the last of the water droplets of rain hitting the birches, and watched the stream swell ever so slightly. Then, as a perfect gift and at a perfect moment, I witnessed the blue heron gracefully sail across the open field fifty yards away, level with my eye, in the background, and at the same time a male hummingbird visited the feeder three feet away. And again, humbled, I realized these are but a few of the myriad mystical connections, between the land, the water, the air, and life, and relished my place in this universe.

I am now focused on renovating the cottage adjacent to the stream hoping to complete this work by December. This work is another journey like others I have taken over forty years and follows a language I speak fluently as an architect who has built. But I selfishly work in the stream two to three days a week continually tuning the water and walking the stream every day to be soothed by her healing energy. So, the journey is never complete, the seeing never darkened, the practice never ending; the doing always leads to more to be done, there is always more to study, and the real courage lies in all of us looking inward without fear of failure or success. What began as a practical mission to save birch trees along the stream, revive continuous water flow and stop bank erosion, grew into much more; a passionate continuing practice, an exposure to a new language and study elevating the work of restoring the stream to art, and holding it in place for my children. Inevitably, I had little choice as the stream beckoned me to her and selfishly, I indulged that primal allure to water. But then, something mystical happened. The physical work I was doing and the meditation in the water led to glorious discoveries, the learning of a new language, the humble understanding of a new reality, and revival and return of life in the stream, represented by the presence of the salamanders.

This enlightenment directly and symbolically manifested in concert with the renewal of my floundering and damaged spirit. The beauty is the practice, the positive evolution of the stream, the work I did in partnership with nature coincided with the positive evolution of my soul. Witnessing the wonders, the meandering stream, the sound of the falls, the riffles, the smell of the spring water, the runs, the pocket waters, the deep holes, the pressure of the water against and around my legs, the leaf-boats of fall riding the currents, the fluid dappled light falling between the birch trees, reinforced the reality that we are all involved in an alive, forever changing, never finishing dance. Rains still come at the whim of nature, boulders the size of Volkswagens still crash to the stream randomly, water in the stream rises to flood levels and falls to normal levels seasonally, smaller boulders shift unpredictably, the stream takes on new forms by the second. The work I have done has assisted the stream to move toward balance, changes are ongoing, with only one absolute—gravity. And it is all magic.

However, at the sunset of this lifetime, one moment, one day, I will be prodded to cease my ongoing work here, by that always uninvited guest, that scythe carrying dancing fool cloaked in a black robe and woolen cowl. Hopefully, I will be standing in the middle of the streambed contemplating the latest changes and new work needing to be done and listening to the voice of the calming riffles singing to me peacefully. Then while washed by the cooling waters' embrace, before I must move one last time, I will try to sway my guest that he should exchange his bladed tool for a fly rod. Reluctantly, I know I must eventually relent and vouchsafe the stream to others to tend. But, with coins on my eyes, as I am ferried downstream, and as I reach the confluence and begin crossing the river Styx, believe me, I will send a message to St. Peter letting him know I will be discussing with Virgil and Charon my new and ongoing plans for re-working the water and suggesting improvements so it will accommodate brook trout, crayfish, freshwater snails and of course the magnificent salamanders.

Work Boots and Gloves by the Wood Stove
Pencil on paper
Mark T. Wright

Acknowledgements

A nd I thought writing the book was difficult! It is impossible to concisely express my gratitude to all the individuals contributing to this effort. As the stream connects the energy of these mountains in the high country of North Carolina to the universe, I have been graced by the threads of energy that I have clung to connecting me to these beautiful individuals.

Patrice Samara, COO of Wordeee. With the patience of Job, she deeply understood me and helped me craft this journal into something tangible while navigating my eccentricities. She encouraged me and told me this book needed to be written. By fate, luck, or a soul contract, I was introduced to her by my dearest friend, Perri Neri, Artist and Director of Living Room-NYC, a creative gallery. A brilliant artist, she has acted as my first critic, subtlety letting me know with loving kindness when the work fell way short but celebrated with me when it rose. Shayna Steinger, who initially encouraged me to take the journal sketching and transform it into a book, and who said to me, surprised, after she read an early draft, "I love it and you can write." My deepest gratitude to Dr. John Gilderbloom, Professor, University of Louisville, Urban and Public Affairs, who recruited me into the PhD program at the university. His energy, kind heart, and intellect are an inspiration to students and other educators. Tony Roccanova, Professor Emeritus of the School of Architecture at the University of Kentucky, who I have known for nearly fifty years. He opened doors to limitless profound possibilities for me and countless students through the art of architecture. Now as a dear friend, I have thanked him countless times, for the foundation he helped lay.

Dr. Joe D'Ambrosia, who listened to me before the stream. Chris Byrd, who began as my intern and now is my colleague and friend, and said, "Doctor, it is time for you to stop suffering." My two oldest friends, Terry Wilson and Mindy Meurer, who have cradled me when life would not. James Daryl Eason and Rob Mullins, who have tolerated me and somehow remained my dear friends. Sam and Patty Wright, peanut m & m's and 7 UP, you know. Nancy LaChapelle, the 'end of a beginning.' Carl Freeman, the fish whisperer who introduced me with insight into the world of North Carolina trout fishing. Traci Artus helped me find this mountain home with the impossible parameters I set for her. The stream, the water, the birch trees, the trout, the crawdads, Bobby, the water snake, and the salamanders, I thank them daily, and they have inspired me to work and allow me to share their world.

Margaret Annie and Harry, I love you with tears. These mountains, the stream, the land, have a sacred inspirational energy I thought could not be amplified. I was wrong. When you are with me here, the mystical magnificence of this place becomes incomprehensibly dazzling. It is a place, a beautiful place, where you two have helped me gather my scattered heart back to one.

About The Author

MarkT.Wright, PhD, AIA, NCARB, is a practicing architect. He received his Doctorate in Urban and Public Affairs, Planning and Development from the University of Louisville. He is the Founder and President of Oracle Design Group and has concentrated his award-winning forty plus year career on developing, designing, and building affordable housing. He also specializes in the renovation and adaptive reuse of historic buildings. He taught Urban Planning and Design at the University of Kentucky, University of Louisville, and University of Cincinnati. Upon moving to the high country of North Carolina, an added focus became the ecologically conscious development, incremental preservation and restoration of priceless stream resources…a passion project. *THE TAIL OF A SALAMANDER* is his first book.